D0906967

Folk Arts and Crafts
of Japan

Volume 26

THE HEIBONSHA SURVEY OF JAPANESE ART

For a list of the entire series see end of book

CONSULTING EDITORS

Katsuichiro Kamei, *art critic*
Seiichiro Takahashi, *Chairman, Japan Art Academy*
Ichimatsu Tanaka, *Chairman, Cultural Properties Protection Commission*

Folk Arts and Crafts of Japan

by KAGEO MURAOKA
and KICHIEMON OKAMURA

translated by Daphne D. Stegmaier

New York · WEATHERHILL/HEIBONSHA · Tokyo

This book was originally published in Japanese by Heibonsha under the title *Mingei* in the Nihon no Bijutsu series. Chapters one, four, and five were written by Kageo Muraoka, the remainder by Kichiemon Okamura. The illustrations were selected by Kageo Muraoka.

First English Edition, 1973

Jointly published by John Weatherhill, Inc., 149 Madison Avenue, New York, New York 10016, with editorial offices at 7-6-13 Roppongi, Minato-ku, Tokyo 106, and Heibonsha, Tokyo. Copyright © 1967, 1973, by Heibonsha; all rights reserved. Printed in Japan.

Library of Congress Cataloging in Publication Data: Muraoka, Kageo, 1901– /Folk arts and crafts of Japan./(The Heibonsha survey of Japanese art) /Translation of Mingei./1. Art industries and trade, Japanese. 2. Folk art—Japan. I. Okamura, Kichiemon, 1916– joint author. II. Title. III. Series./NK1071.M8713/745'.0952/72–78600/ISBN 0–8348–1009–3

78574

Contents

Folk Arts and Crafts
of Japan

The Hidden Beauty of Common Objects

THE CRAFTSMAN AND HIS CRAFT Soetsu Yanagi* (1889–1961) was one of the founders of Japanese folk-art theory and a former director of the Nihon Mingeikan (Japan Folk Crafts Museum) in Tokyo. In an article written in 1926 entitled "Zakki no Bi" (The Beauty of Common Objects) he described the folk artisan and his relation to his work as follows:

"Although the Japanese folk artisan is poor and uneducated, he is a fervent devotee of his craft. While it is difficult for him to describe fully what he believes in, his surprising personal experiences are clearly expressed in the crude vocabulary of his work. And even though there is nothing unique or rare about his artistic technique, the essence of his creed is reflected in the objects he creates. Unconsciously, he is motivated by his belief in *kami* (the spirit of nature) and seized by its indomitable force.

"I can say the same thing concerning this dish that now absorbs my attention. It might seem to be something scorned as a poor or clumsily made object, since it is lacking in extravagant elegance and ornate stylization. Because he was not self-conscious

about what he was doing, the man who made this dish had not planned the final outcome of his creative effort. As though he were a passionate believer repeatedly chanting a god's name, he forms the same shape on the potter's wheel again and again, and time after time he paints the same picture on the vessel using the same glaze.

"What is beauty? What is the art of the kiln? We cannot expect him to be prepared with clear-cut answers to such questions, but even though he may not have a thought-out knowledge, his hands move rapidly at his work. And we could perhaps say that just as the voice that speaks the Buddha's name is not actually the man's voice but is that of the Buddha, so too the hands of the potter are not his own but are those of nature. Rather than the craftsman directing the work, it is nature that comes and protects its beauty. The craftsman has forgotten all worldly cares. As belief grows out of selfless immersion in faith, beauty springs forth spontaneously in the vessel he makes. His creation thus holds me in rapt absorption."

Perhaps the plate Soetsu Yanagi was describing was a *nishime* plate (used for hard-boiled fish and vegetables) produced in Seto (in Aichi Prefecture), with a pattern of pinks (Fig. 4).

Folk-craft products, of which this plate is repre-

---

*The names of all modern (post-1868) Japanese in this book are given, as in this case, in Western style (surname last); those of all premodern Japanese are given in Japanese style (surname first).

1 (far left). Tokkuri: *sakè de-canter. Porcelain; height, 22 cm. Seventeenth century. Imari, Saga Prefecture. Japan Folk Crafts Museum, Tokyo.*

2 (left). Tokkuri: *sakè decanter. Porcelain; height, 20.5 cm. Nineteenth century. Hirasa, Kagoshima Prefecture. Kumamoto International Folk Crafts Museum, Kumamoto Prefecture.*

3. Wan: *bowl. Porcelain; height,* ▷
8 cm. Eighteenth century. Imari, Saga Prefecture. Collection of Toyotaro Tanaka, Tokyo.

sentative, are beautiful objects that were reasonably priced and were used in ancient times by the common people in their kitchens. Consequently, they were looked down upon. Their beauty was not deliberately aimed at, nor were they expensive items like those displayed in a tokonoma alcove. These are, instead, vessels of the kind sold at ordinary kitchenware shops and used in ordinary kitchens.

Common folk objects include not only plates, bowls, teapots, earthenware bottles, trays, chests, and garments, like raincoats and straw coats to keep out the cold, but also various other utensils used for labor. These are objects that are necessary in the everyday lives of ordinary people. Just as we did not pay attention to the air we breathed before pollution became an issue, so too these commonplace

objects were too familiar to their users to deserve special attention. People thought of them simply in terms of their daily functional value. They did not give much thought to other uses to which they could be put, and when the utensils were no longer fit for their intended use, they were simply thrown away. Moreover, the users did not reflect on their aesthetic nature or where their beauty sprang from or how that beauty had been put to use. Perhaps it was natural for them to be left unnoticed in those days when they were so commonplace as to be found in every home. Even among historians and scholars who specialized in aesthetics, there was no one who appreciated them until recent years. It was, in fact, Soetsu Yanagi who first came to appreciate their beauty. Moreover, for him, they ex-

hibited not just another form of beauty: to his perceptive eyes, it was the supreme beauty. And his intelligence led him to learn what this beauty is and where it comes from.

MINGEI DEFINED   According to Soetsu Yanagi, the new word *mingei* is used to describe utilitarian art objects with popular appeal. These everyday articles, which were once looked down upon as "low-class," were first called *mingei* (folk crafts) at the end of the Taisho era (1912–26). However, this followed more than a decade's accumulation of insight and speculation extending from the end of the Meiji era (1868–1912) through the Taisho era. Thus it has been almost fifty years since the term *mingei* came into use. Throughout this period, and in accordance with changing social and historical conditions, the word *mingei* has been used with a variety of meanings, its scope being broadened to cover things that are far from the original meaning of the word. At one time, *mingei* was confused with farmers' arts and was even considered to be a branch of ethnic art.

As Soetsu Yanagi noted, however, the word *mingei* means popular, utilitarian arts. These are not works of art that express beauty alone: they can never be separated from their practical aspect, through which they express a natural beauty. They comprise, of course, a different kind of art from pure fine arts, in which the prime consideration is the pursuit of beauty. Thus it comes under the category sometimes referred to as applied art or

4. Ishi-zara: *stone-glazed plate. Diameter, 27 cm. Nineteenth century. Seto, Aichi Prefecture. Japan Folk Crafts Museum, Tokyo.*

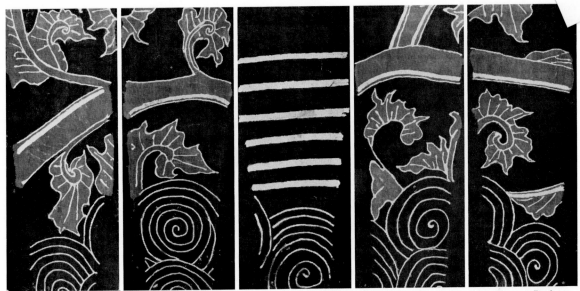

5. Shishimai-isho: *material for costume of the lion-dance (a type of folk dance). Cotton. Twentieth century. Toyama Prefecture. Toyama City Folk Crafts Museum, Toyama Prefecture.*

nonfree art. Moreover, *mingei* must be distinguished from the decorative artistic applied arts of the aristocracy, which, while utilitarian, place their major emphasis on aesthetic impact. Folk articles are everyday, functional objects whose principal aim is to fulfill the needs of ordinary people. They are not special or valuable objects.

Each such object carries the weight of long tradition, reflecting the times and environments and life styles of its users. Thus, they are significant as symbols of the people's traditions and feelings. These commonplace, functional artifacts are endowed with a beauty directly connected with their utility. Their beauty is neither remarkable nor magnificent, but simple, humble, and unassuming.

The word *mingei* was coined to describe the discovery of this kind of beauty and the everyday objects that express it. Therefore *mingei*, while it refers to one domain of utilitarian art under the heading of applied art, is a word originally used with a solemn, particular value of beauty. When it

becomes necessary to coin a word, it is because a meaning that cannot be expressed by existing words has been discovered. The word *mingei* came into use at about the time of the announcement in 1926 of the planned construction of a Japan folk crafts museum. This date marks the new consciousness of the beauty and value of ordinary utilitarian objects. The first appeal to society for recognition of this new aesthetic approach was Yanagi's *Kogei no Michi* (The Way of Crafts), published in 1927.

The foregoing does not mean that the worth of folk artifacts had gone completely unrecognized in former times. During the Momoyama period (1568–1603), such pioneers of the tea ceremony as Murata Juko, Takeno Jo-o, and Sen no Rikyu did recognize this beauty, and upon it they founded *wabi-no-chado* (the tea ceremony of rustic simplicity).

Among the articles used in their tea ceremony were Chinese *t'ien-mu* (in Japanese, *temmoku*) tea bowls and caddies, as well as Korean tea bowls of the Koryo style. The Chinese utensils were of a type

6. Katsugi: *garment formerly worn by women over head and shoulders to hide the face (for instance at weddings or as a sign of mourning). Asa; length, 115 cm. Nineteenth century. Shonai area, Yamagata Prefecture. Japan Folk Crafts Museum, Tokyo.*

originally in common use at monasteries on T'ien-mu-shan, a sacred Buddhist mountain in China's Fukien Province, where the bowls had been used for medicinal tea and the caddies had originally been used as medicine jars. It is widely recognized today that powdered-tea bowls called *Ido-jawan* and revered as representing the finest Koryo-style ware were used by the common people as rice bowls in the early part of the Yi dynasty (1392–1910). Much pottery called *o-meibutsu* (famous specialties) was originally considered commonplace, and it was the tea-ceremony masters who first recognized its beauty. Along with the high development of the *tocha* (tea-guessing competition) and the *shoin-no-cha* (guest-room tea ceremony), which flourished during the Muromachi period (1336–

1568), it was regarded as prestigious to be a good judge of tea utensils, and this encouraged the importation of expensive and rare articles chosen by connoisseurs. But the taste of the early tea masters did not lean toward such valuable and showy objects. Instead, they preferred unsigned, humble, commonplace articles. Moreover, they discovered exceedingly beautiful things among them. When a utensil conforms to its intended usage, its intrinsic beauty stands out most clearly: the essence of a utensil's existence lies in its utility. The deep perception of these pioneer tea masters is evident in the fact that they judged a utensil not only by viewing it in terms of visual beauty alone but also by considering it in terms of its functionality. Because of their deep appreciation, the tea masters even went

7. Funa-dansu: *seaman's chest.*
Wood and iron; height, 50.5 cm.
Nineteenth century. Collection of
Shoji Hamada, Tochigi Prefecture.

so far as to bestow on these everyday utensils the title of *o-meibutsu*. These founders of the tea ceremony used rice bowls created by unnamed Korean craftsmen as tea bowls in the *wabi-no-chado*. Thus it was through the early tea-ceremony masters that commonplace objects first acquired admirers.

However, whether the founders of the tea ceremony actually realized that these tasteful utensils were originally insignificant, everyday wares is debatable. Probably they were not concerned with such matters and therefore were not concerned about why these objects were beautiful or how it was that they could have been made so beautifully. To the Japanese, the beauty of nature or of man-made things seemed to be a matter of course, and people simply enjoyed it. This has been the tradi-

tion of aesthetic consciousness since ancient times in Japan. Generally speaking, the consideration of the principles of beauty apart from beautiful things themselves was first introduced to Japan from the West. The Japanese in general did not judge tangibly beautiful objects by following some theory of aesthetics until their attitudes changed conspicuously after the introduction of Western customs. This is noted by Soetsu Yanagi in his *Sakumotsu no Kohansei* (The Later Life of Artifacts):

"Things are chosen by their appearance and become a part of life through their use. These two aspects comprise a world of appreciation, of enjoyment, and this enjoyment of life must have reached its consummation in the early development of the tea ceremony. However, those of us who live in

8. Bon: *tray. Lacquered wood; 29 × 27.8 cm. Nineteenth century. Wagatani, Ishikawa Prefecture. Collection of Shoji Hamada, Tochigi Prefecture.*

9. Jizaikagi: *pothook. Wood and iron; length, 43.5 cm. Nineteenth century. Kanazawa, Ishikawa Prefecture. Japan Folk Crafts Museum, Tokyo.*

this era of consciousness have a new responsibility toward the utensils: to think about their beauty aside from just looking at and appreciating them. The utensils now come into our own consciousness, our thought. The recognition of beauty has created new chores for modern man. It is the kind of work the tea men had not gone into adequately in their time. It is a new pleasure possible only in our era of consciousness. Artifacts become valuable only through recognition: they are not to be simply looked at and used; their raison d'être, deeply hidden during ancient times, can be made explicit by reflecting on them. Thinking men's artifacts are a product of modern times. In this sense, the tea-ceremony men are not to be regarded as thinkers."

Here Soetsu Yanagi shows a warm and deep understanding of the forerunners of the tea ceremony as well as a sharply critical attitude toward their limitations. At the same time he reveals his own attitude as a modern man toward the theme of beauty, especially in regard to folk art.

A FOLK-CRAFT THEORY Soetsu Yanagi was born in 1889 and died in 1961. The fact that he grew to manhood during late Meiji and early Taisho cannot be ignored, for the age was one whose important historical and social developments contributed to the discovery of the beauty of folk crafts and to the formulation of his own aesthetic theory. Awed by Western civilization, the Japanese of the Meiji era devoted themselves to absorbing and uncritically following Western culture with its modern spirit based upon reason and will, and the self-awareness and inde-

10. Otsu-e: *painting of the god Hachiman Daibosatsu. Colors on paper; 31.5 × 17.2 cm. Seventeenth century. Otsu, Shiga Prefecture. Japan Folk Crafts Museum, Tokyo.*

11. O-bachi: *large bowl. Porcelain; diameter, 47 cm. Seventeenth century. Kutani, Ishikawa Prefecture. Japan Folk Crafts Museum, Tokyo.*

12. Furoshiki: *cloth used for wrapping and carrying things. Abacá; approximately 115 cm. square. Nineteenth century. Naha, Okinawa Prefecture. Kurashiki Folk Crafts Museum, Okayama Prefecture.*

13. Nobori: *detail of banner. Cotton. Eighteenth century. Matsue,* ▷
Shimane Prefecture. Collection of Keisuke Serisawa, Tokyo.

14. Rindai: *stand for bell used in religious worship. Lacquered wood; height, 9.3 cm. Seventeenth century. Collection of Shoji Hamada, Tochigi Prefecture.*

15. Funa-dansu: *detail of sea chest. Wood and iron; height, 36.3 cm. Eighteenth century. Collection of Shoji Hamada, Tochigi Prefecture.*

16. Funa-dokkuri: wide-bottomed sakè decanter. Earthenware; height, 37 cm. Seventeenth century. Kamaya, Hyogo Prefecture. Japan Folk Crafts Museum, Tokyo.

17. Suibyo: water container. Earthenware; height, 25 cm. Seventeenth century. Seto, Aichi Prefecture. Collection of Shoji Hamada, Tochigi Prefecture.

pendence of man. Moreover, the Japanese were driven by impatience to catch up and achieve the same kinds of "miracles" that had been produced by this culture. They followed the trends of the new era, ignoring and discarding everything connected with the past. Absorbing Western culture amid this new stream of thought, Soetsu Yanagi was now in a better position to deepen his awareness of the Orient and of Japan through the mediation of a Western intellect. Guided by a spirit that searched constantly for the superb, he could not help noticing the intrinsic values and truths hidden in things that were about to be discarded. He thus discovered folk art through intuition, and influenced by Western thinking, he formulated his own theories based on a deeper realization of the worth of the Oriental spirit.

But theories about folk crafts did not begin with abstract aesthetic speculations. Nor were they theories that aspired to a transcendental ideal of beauty isolated from concrete objects. These common objects first began as dusty, hand-stained articles. They were accepted and evaluated as such without appeal to any authority; indeed they were looked down upon. That is to say, they began first as "objects," the beauty of which was then recognized, and this understanding progressed finally to the point where there came an intellectual curiosity as to what made these objects beautiful and, beyond this, to a theoretical explication of their beauty.

An indomitable belief in truth, beauty, and faith as a unity underlay the life of Soetsu Yanagi. He rejected the dualistic view of value, such as good or bad, beautiful or ugly, authentic or spurious. He

18. Kame: *crock. Earthenware; height, 20 cm. Seventeenth century. Tachikui, Hyogo Prefecture.
Japan Folk Crafts Museum, Tokyo.*

attempted to gain insight into that which lay between opposing values found in a dualistic world.
He stood for a unity that had overcome all opposition. His was a stand without a stand, a matter of
direct and pure intuition. For him, the superb was
manifested not in speculation or meditation but in
directly observing actual creations of folk crafts.
Objects possess a beauty that surpasses beauty and

ugliness. Through intuition, he was able to perceive unique beauty in such a commonplace object as a plate.

In this way, a hitherto unnoticed beauty was
found in the utensils that fulfilled various uses in
the everyday life of the common people in Japan.
This beauty was the unique beauty not only of folk
art but also of all that is beautiful.

CHAPTER TWO

Folk-Craft Products

CERAMICS The first step in the making of a ceramic utensil is to mold the form out of clay, after which the form is fixed by firing in a kiln. Because of the nature of the materials used and the techniques of firing, very large objects cannot be made. Tableware is the most common field of application for ceramics. Ceramic products range in size from small sakè cups and chopstick rests to small and medium-sized plates, rice bowls, soup bowls, noodle bowls, *hachi* (various vessels of the bowl type; Figs. 19, 20, 30, 111, 139), water pitchers, *kasane* (sets of stackable containers), small pitchers for soy sauce, condiment containers, tea bowls (Figs. 109, 110), *dobin* (teapots; Figs. 32, 149), *kyusu* (small teapots used at the table; Fig. 118), cups for Western-style tea and coffee, cake plates, fruit plates, and decanters and other sakè utensils. Ceramic articles are so widely used that it is impossible to imagine a meal without them. Because they come in many different shapes—circular shapes, square shapes, leaf shapes, fish shapes, etc. —there is great variety in ceramic tableware. Ceramics for cooking purposes include such kitchen ware as: *katakuchi* (lipped) bowls (Fig. 101), kneading bowls (Fig. 96), pots, bowls for roasting tea leaves, charcoal stoves, *kamado* (hollow rectangular utensils; the inside is a fire chamber and cooking is done in a vessel placed over an opening in the top), and crocks (Fig. 95) for storing water used to douse cooking fires. Until very recently, crocks for storage purposes were necessary. Large crocks with wide mouths are called *kame* (Figs. 18, 80, 81, 140, 141); tall crocks whose lower half is a little narrower than the upper part are called *hando-game*; *tsubo* (Figs. 24, 95, 97, 103, 104, 151, 152) are smaller than *kame*. Most *tsubo* are narrow toward the mouth, although there is one kind with the same diameter from top to bottom called *kittate*. *Tsubo* with lids are called *futatsubo*, while small *tsubo* with small mouths are called *bin* (bottle). *Tokkuri* (sakè decanter) originally was not a Japanese word but was borrowed from the Korean. *Tokkuri* come in various shapes and sizes depending on their use (Figs. 2, 28, 29, 83, 84, 108). Other ceramic wares include *suiteki* (a small water container used in calligraphy) and a considerable variety of festival and flower-arrangement utensils. Also a wide variety of ceramic products such as well rims, roof tiles, wall tiles, and certain pieces of fishing equipment are fired in kilns.

Ceramic ware is very popular in Japan, and there is probably no other country that produces a greater variety of fired articles. Even after excluding the very important tea utensils, there remains an abundance and variety of tableware that can be found nowhere else in the world. When comparing the utensils used in serving Japanese food with those used for Western or Chinese food, many differences become apparent. For example, Western tableware centers on plates. Japanese plates, unlike those found in the West, are slightly curved and not completely flat at the bottom. Curves are

the natural shapes for ceramic ware, as complex techniques are necessary for the making of flat-bottomed plates. Flat plates are vestiges of the metal plates used in the West before ceramic ware came into widespread use. Chinese tableware is centered on large bowls supplemented by plates and smaller bowls, whereas in Japanese tableware small bowls and plates are most commonly used with large bowls being supplementary. The Koreans use medium-sized bowls both with and without covers, but rarely make use of plates.

During the Edo period when each daimyo's fief was economically self-sufficient, the people in each area were encouraged to build their own local kilns. Glazed ceramics were made in Seto (near present Nagoya) and then spread to other places. A wide variety of products was produced and the artisans experimented with many techniques. There are various ways of categorizing ceramic products, and one widely used method is based on the kind of material used. Thus we have porcelain made from *jido* (kaolin) and earthenware made from *nendo*

(plain clay) or *todo* (potter's clay). Potter's clay results after years of weathering causes the gradual decomposition of feldspar, quartz, and granite. The resulting soluble materials are carried off and deposited in various locations.

There are two types of potter's clay found in Seto that are well known for their high quality. *Kibushi* (literally, wood knot) is a clay containing organic matter that blackens when fired. It sometimes contains fossils of roots, hence the name. The other type is called *gairome*, or frog's eye, as the clay contains imbedded quartz flecks that when wet shine like a frog's eyes. *Gairome* containing only a small amount of iron turns whitish when fired. Potter's clay contains organic fibers that lend a plasticity essential for ease in molding, and the metallic elements such as iron that are present produce warm, black tones in the coloring of the finished product.

Kaolin contains the same basic minerals as potter's clay and accumulates in similar places, but kaolin has been further broken down by me-

19. Sekisho-bachi: *bowl. Earthenware; diameter, 33 cm. Nineteenth century. Fushina, Shimane Prefecture. Tottori Folk Crafts Museum, Tottori Prefecture.*

20. O-bachi: *large bowl. Earthenware; diameter, 42.5 cm. Nineteenth century. Niwaki, Saga Prefecture. Collection of Shoji Hamada, Tochigi Prefecture.*

chanical action and the effects of carbonic acid and water. Japan's best kaolin is found in Amakusa (Nagasaki Prefecture, Kyushu) and in Saijo (Hiroshima Prefecture). Objects made from potter's clay are sometimes called *tsuchimono* (earthenware), while those made from kaolin are called *ishimono* (stoneware) or *shiro kiji* (white body). Porcelain articles are fired at high temperatures and they make a beautiful, clear sound when tapped. Held up to the light, the thin part at the bottom of porcelain ware appears translucent. Porcelain bowls and dishes are widely used because porcelain ware gives a feeling of cleanliness.

All porcelain is glazed, but this is not true of all earthenware. Most unglazed pottery is fired at low temperatures, a technique that goes far back in history. This type of ware, called *doki* (literally, "earthenware") or *gaki* (literally, "tile ware"), though easily broken, is heat resistant. Unglazed articles that are fired at high temperatures are sometimes referred to as *sekki* or *jiki*. High-fired unglazed articles include vessels for roasting tea

leaves or beans, *tsubo, hibachi* (charcoal braziers), hand and foot warmers, *kamado*, religious utensils (Fig. 153), and roof tiles. All of these objects were very important in the daily lives of the common people. Among more unusual articles are *tako tsubo* (pots for catching octopus), *haze tsubo* (earthenware pots for trapping goby fish; Fig. 151), and various fishing sinkers.

Glazes are the clothes and cosmetics of ceramics. The various colors of the glasslike glazes are an important characteristic of ceramics. These glazes not only enhance the beauty of the finished article but have the important functions of protection against breakage and making the objects nonporous. Among the glazes used in Japan, *hai-gusuri* (ash glazes) are the most popular. Potters discovered that when ash from the wood used for firing settled on a pot and fused, it took on the appearance of glass, so they started applying ash purposely. Because the ash glaze itself is transparent, soil containing iron, copper, or other metals is often mixed in to give color. The resulting glazes

21. Sara: *plate. Porcelain; diameter 12.5 cm. Eighteenth century. Hasami, Nagasaki Prefecture. Collection of Toyotaro Tanaka, Tokyo.*

are called *tetsu-gusuri* (iron glaze) and *do-gusuri* (copper glaze), etc. These glazes produce various color effects that are categorized as follows: *temmoku* (a black glaze with metallic tones), *kaki* (orange glaze), *ame* (a brownish glaze), *soba* (a grayish white glaze), and *irabo* (various shades of brown ranging from yellow ocher to dark brown in which the glaze forms a net pattern). Lead glaze, which is relatively rare in Japan, is a substance that melts at a lower temperature than ash glaze. Iron and copper are also mixed in to give metallic color effects similar to those of ash glaze.

The glaze used on earthenware is usually thicker than that of porcelain, and it contains small cracks *(kannyu)* and bubbles. The bubbles allow a diffusion of light that imparts a special softness to the finished object. Pottery made of clay containing iron is liable to take on a metallic color, and to

avoid this the body is covered with a white slip (liquid clay) and the glaze is applied over this. Articles made by this process are called *shirae-gake* or *kesho-gake*. This technique was first used in the kilns of northern Kyushu and then spread throughout the country; the "soft" and beautiful utensils made in Okinawa (Figs. 83, 102) are fine examples of it. In *namako* glaze, the metals used to bring out the colors are not uniformly mixed, so that on firing subtle patches of color appear in the finished product (Figs. 19, 30). Large numbers of these articles are found in the northern prefectures.

An immense variety of drip-glazes has been devised by Japanese artisans. In the *nagashi-gusuri* glazing technique, loam and white clay are mixed with metals that will produce white, black, blue, green, yellow, or red tones, and the mixture is then poured on the article and allowed to flow

22. Sobachoko: *cup for sauce in which* soba *noodles are dipped. Porcelain; height, 6 cm. Nineteenth century. Imari, Saga Prefecture. Collection of Toyotaro Tanaka, Tokyo.*

(Figs. 16, 18, 20, 28, 80, 85, 106, 107, 141). In Seto, small lumps of copper are put on the edge of *hachi* and plates. On firing, these melt and flow, producing a "soft" effect. This may be regarded as an early form of drip-technique. Drip-glazes suited Japanese tastes and the various kilns developed their own distinctive techniques. In Tamba, Hyogo Prefecture, an unevenness is created on the shoulders of vessels by using a bamboo tube filled with glaze, the upper end of which is covered with a finger. Finger movement controls the flow of the glaze. This method is sometimes used with other techniques, and it has led to the devising of many other methods. In the field of Japanese ceramics *nagashi-gusuri* methods exhibit tremendous variety and have an importance that cannot be ignored.

Porcelain glaze is transparent and does not contain bubbles or cracks, for here the object is to emphasize the whiteness of the body. Potters have tried out many kinds of wood ash for porcelain glazes, but the most favored glaze is made with the ash of the *isu-no-ki*, a tree belonging to the witch hazel family. This glaze has proved to be the best, giving a soft, gentle effect.

Besides *hakuji*, or plain white porcelain (Figs. 2, 31, 32), there is *sometsuke*, decorated porcelain. This name came from *ai-zome*, an indigo textile dyeing technique. Potters originally drew patterns with a clear blue pigment over the glaze, but later the patterns were drawn directly on the body and then coated with glaze. Asbolite, an earthy material containing manganese cobalt oxides, was one of the pigments used. Among the objects decorated by this method were *tsubo*, large *hachi* (Fig. 139), sakè decanters (Figs. 1, 108), and a variety of other vessels ranging from flower vases to sakè cups.

23. Meshi-wan: *rice bowl. Porcelain; height, 6 cm. Eighteenth century. Imari, Saga Prefecture. Collection of Toyotaro Tanaka, Tokyo.*

Sometsuke with a typically Japanese flavor are represented by Imari tea bowls (Figs. 109, 110), *soba* cups (Fig. 22), sakè cups, rice bowls (Fig. 23), noodle bowls, and dishes. Among these the most satisfying are wares called *kurawanka* (Figs. 3, 21). They have a center circle left unglazed, to enable them to be stacked on one another during firing. Imari ware uses a great variety of Japanese-style patterns, and, because it is easy to draw on the small sakè and *soba* cups, over a thousand designs have been created for use on them. Besides Imari, areas of production include Kutani, Seto, and Tobe (in Aichi Prefecture).

Porcelain and *sometsuke* are inseparably related. Techniques originating in China entered northern Kyushu by way of Korea, and during the Edo period the methods of firing and painting porcelain that were introduced brought about great changes

in everyday tableware. The articles were transported by ship to various parts of Japan and used widely throughout the country. Apart from a small number of early examples printed from blocks, all designs were drawn by hand. A paint brush held in the hand of a skillful painter produced free, refreshing, and bright designs.

In the *aka-e* technique, designs in red, yellow, green, deep blue, or purple are drawn on the hardened body after firing. The designs are then fixed by refiring the vessel at a low temperature. The name *aka-e* literally means "red picture," but the pattern is not necessarily always drawn in red. *Aka-e* has become popular because it contains various colors and makes the table look very gay. As the designs are applied after firing, the ware is sometimes called *uwa-e* ("over-picture"). For *aka-e* also, Imari (Figs. 82, 112) and Kutani wares (Figs.

24. Tsubo: *crock. Porcelain; height, 11 cm. Seventeenth century. Kutani, Ishikawa Prefecture. Japan Folk Crafts Museum, Tokyo.*

11, 24) are representative. Imari ware presents a freshness resembling *yuzen* textile patterns, while Kutani ware has a solemn character and a feeling of strength, reflecting the differences between the southern and the northern prefectures. *Aka-e* designs are not simply borrowed from textiles and lacquerware. They are in a style not to be seen in pure painting, and have a beauty of brushwork different from that of *sometsuke,* where the design is applied to a highly absorbent surface. *Aka-e* patterns are found on some Okinawan pottery and on Banko ware (predominantly red articles that originated in Ise, Mie Prefecture), but they are undoubtedly best suited to porcelain. *Aka-e* designs are valued both in combination with *sometsuke* and on their own.

Designs on porcelain can be painted by hand; for example, the cobalt blue *sometsuke* designs and the *aka-e.* Pottery, however, because of its texture shows few detailed drawings in comparison with the great number found on porcelain ware. Very simple drawings are more suitable for pottery. When the use of iron pigments increased, these decorations were called *tetsu-e* (Fig. 29), or iron pictures. *Tetsu-e* originated in Seto, and from this tradition came the *ishi-zara* (stone-glazed plates; Figs. 4, 26, 105) and the plates to hold paper-covered oil lanterns (Figs. 25, 79). The beauty of this ware is due to its generous brush strokes. Asbolite is always added to these rough pottery dishes. Large deep plates of about 14 to 16 inches in diameter (Fig. 154), made in Kasahara, Gifu Prefecture, during the Momoyama period, are good examples. Both the above-mentioned ceramics and those from northern Kyushu have a green color due to copper, which gives them a particular charm.

25. Andon-zara: *plate placed under an oil lantern. Earthenware; diameter, 22.5 cm. Eighteenth century. Seto, Aichi Prefecture. Collection of Kanjiro Kawai, Kyoto.*

The methods of making patterns on clay are different from those used in drawing ordinary pictures. For example, there is *ronuki,* a wax-resist method resembling the batik dyeing technique. *Yubi-gaki* (finger-combing) patterns made with the fingers on a *shirae-gake* (white slip) while still wet (Fig. 142), and *kushi-gaki,* patterns made with combs (Fig. 20), are frequently seen in northern Kyushu. There are also incised drawings and carvings called *kugi-bori* (Fig. 83), done with nails and other implements. There is an endless variety of techniques: *kakiotoshi,* the scraping and partial cutting away of parts of the body; *tobiganna,* wavy patterns made with a carpenter's plane (Fig. 111); *itchin,* the pressing out of slips, etc., from a tube (Figs. 27, 104); *zogan,* or colored-clay inlay; nega-

tive and positive stamped designs (Fig. 152); *haritsuke,* the addition of long narrow clay cords (Fig. 97); the method of putting clay onto boards to obtain grain imprints; and the method of splashing glaze. These techniques, unlimited in number, did not aim at the portrayal of pictures. There is also *hakeme,* the application of a white slip with a brush. These techniques are often seen in northern Kyushu. Sometimes the *uchibake* technique of slapping with a large brush is used (Fig. 148), and *mado-e* designs, found on jars and vases (Fig. 103), are made by partially dipping the side of the pot into a white slip.

Nowadays there are automatic electric and oil-fired kilns. These came to be used in order to increase firing efficiency and economize on fuel.

26. Ishi-zara: *stone-glazed plate. Diameter, 27.3 cm. Nineteenth century. Seto, Aichi Prefecture. Collection of Shoji Hamada, Tochigi Prefecture.*

The earliest method of firing in the open air was improved upon and the closed furnace was devised. Then by utilizing the slopes of hillsides, holes were dug and *ana-gama,* cavelike kilns, were devised. These underground kilns then developed into *mizo-gama,* a trench-type kiln, whose lower half remained underground, while the upper half protruded and was covered with a roof. These were followed by *nobori-gama,* climbing kilns, which are completely above ground and run uphill. The *mizo-gama* have disappeared, but the *teppo-gama,* which reflect the transition from the *mizo-gama* to the *nobori-gama,* can still be seen at Tachikui in Tamba, Hyogo Prefecture. The long and sloping *nobori-gama* allow efficient utilization of the heat from firewood burned in the firebox at the lower end of the kiln.

This type of kiln was developed in East Asia, and most of the traditional Japanese kilns were developments based on this pattern. Even today we can find these kilns at Mashiko, and in Onda, Oita Prefecture, where traditional ceramics are fired. A fine example is Seto's *hongyo,* a huge traditional kiln in the Seto area equipped with ladders that can fire over 10,000 pieces.

A type of kiln that encloses the fire, called *tan-gama* (single-chamber kiln) in Japanese, was developed in the West. Many kilns are being converted to this type in order to economize on fuel. Kilns of the *tan-gama* type were used for firing the *oke suyaki* of Kyoto (small *suyaki,* or unglazed pottery for use in miniature shrines as vessels for offerings), and the small *kin-gama* kilns used for refiring *aka-e* wares to

fix the overglaze decoration also come into this category. (In the *kin-gama* the wood is burned between the outer and inner shells of the kiln chamber.) The most common *tan-gama* are the *kawara-gama*, which are used to fire tiles.

Firing is done either directly or indirectly. The *nobori-gama* is an indirect-firing kiln, while the *kin-gama* is an example of the former. Kilns in various parts of the country vary in size and structure as well as in the angle of slope. These differences cause subtle variations in the firing process and as a result determine the special features of the finished articles. Any type of fuel can be used in heating the kilns, provided it raises the temperature high enough. In Japan red pine, approximately thirty years in age, is favored because it burns with a long flame and gives a high temperature.

Great changes take place in pots during firing. The pots are dried in the sun before being placed in the kiln, but they still contain water of hydration. During firing the pots shrink by about twenty percent due to the loss of this water of hydration, and the clay permanently loses its plasticity. The shape of the pots thus becomes fixed. The resulting colors of the body and glazes vary greatly, depending on whether the flames have an oxidizing or reducing effect. Indeed, so great is the influence of the nature of the flames that expressions like "baptism of fire" and "the magic of flames" have been used in reference to firing. The brightly burning oxidizing flames contain a surplus of oxygen which reacts with the body and glaze of the pot, whereas reducing flames, smoky and deficient in oxygen, take oxygen away from the body and glaze of the

27 (opposite page, left). Tokkuri: sakè decanter. Earthenware; height, 20.5 cm. Nineteenth century. Koishihara, Fukuoka Prefecture. Kumamoto International Folk Crafts Museum, Kumamoto Prefecture.

28 (opposite page, right). Tokkuri: sakè decanter. Earthenware; height, 17 cm. Nineteenth century. Ryumonji, Kagoshima Prefecture. Tottori Folk Crafts Museum, Tottori Prefecture.

29. O-tokkuri: large sakè decanter. Earthenware; height, 31 cm. Eighteenth century. Seto, Aichi Prefecture. Japan Folk Crafts Museum, Tokyo.

pot. During firing, the glaze begins to melt and covers the pot with a thin film. At this point the iron in the glaze takes on a red tinge in the case of oxidizing flames, while with reducing flames a green color results. The color of celadon wares is obtained by this latter process. Metals change color on firing, and copper exhibits the most striking change, becoming green on oxidation and red on reduction. So great are the differences between the two colors that it is hard to believe that they originate from the same substance. Western ceramics generally employ the oxidation process, but in the Orient the reduction process is widely used. When fuel is placed in the kilns by hand, both oxidation and reduction occur, resulting in different effects in different parts of the kiln, or even on different sides of the same piece. Such kilns produce wares rich in complex effects. The older the kiln the greater the likelihood of this happening, and kilns belonging to the common people tended to be of this type. Naeshirogawa *yaki*, first made in Naeshirogawa, Kagoshima Prefecture, Kyushu, by a Korean named Bokuhei, is a good example of such ceramic ware (Figs. 97, 142).

A pot can be shaped by hand, with a potter's wheel (Fig. 117), or with molds. Needless to say, at first all ceramics were formed by hand. As examples we have Jomon pottery and *haniwa* clay figurines. Made in a variety of shapes and designs, they exhibit much spontaneity. Even today, many pieces of a sculptural nature are still molded by hand. The *suiteki* (small water containers for calligraphy) of Seto, made from Momoyama until early Edo, are an example of such ware.

30. Tsukemono-bachi: *bowl used to make pickles. Earthenware; height, 19.5 cm. Nineteenth century. Takato, Nagano Prefecture. Matsumoto Folk Crafts Museum, Nagano Prefecture.*

31 *(opposite page, left).* Hana-ike: *flower vase.* ▷ *Porcelain; height, 14.5 cm. Nineteenth century. Hirasa, Kagoshima Prefecture. Kumamoto International Folk Crafts Museum, Kumamoto Prefecture.*

32 *(opposite page, right).* Dobin: *teapot. Porcelain; height, 11 cm. Nineteenth century. Hirasa, Kagoshima Prefecture. Collection of Shoji Hamada, Tochigi Prefecture.* ▷

The potter's wheel, introduced by way of Korea, made it possible to shape ceramics efficiently and it is still used today. Shaping a piece on a rotating potter's wheel is a dynamic process whereby a pot with a round cross-section is gradually built up in a continuous operation. There are two types of potter's wheel: one is the kick-wheel, which is rotated by foot and came to Japan from Korea, and the other is the hand-wheel, which is operated by hand and came from China. Traditionally, wheels were rotated clockwise. The use of the kick-wheel spread from northern Kyushu to other areas, and that of the hand-wheel began in Seto and then spread to kilns making wares in the Seto tradition. Thus information about the type of wheel used enables us to trace the history of a particular kiln.

Plaster is used to make molds today, but in earlier times molds were made from wood or clay. Pots were shaped by rolling clay out into flat sheets and fitting them against the mold. Complicated parts, such as the spouts and handles of teapots and so on, were made separately and put on later. There are two types of molds, the bowl-shaped mold and the melon-shaped mold. In the bowl type, the upper and lower portions are fitted together, whereas in the melon type, the right- and the left-hand portions come together vertically. The horizontal joints on the shoulder and body of *tsubo* result from using the bowl-type mold, and because assembly simply involves pressing the upper portion down upon the lower portion, the bowl-type mold is the more widely used. Patterns are often engraved on molds so that the ceramic can be

decorated at the same time. Molds come in many shapes and can be used for all kinds of articles. With items like dolls, which sometimes have to be made in sets of as nearly as possible identical pieces, only molds can give the required consistency. Bowl-type and melon-type molds are spoken of as *nuki-gata* (molds from which articles are removed). There is also the *hanjo* mold, which is a combination-type mold used in *ikomi* (a pouring or casting method in which the clay is poured into the molds). *Nishin-bachi*, produced at the Hongo kiln in Fukushima Prefecture, northern Honshu, is an example of objects made from *hanjo* molds. In Tobe, located in Ehime Prefecture on Shikoku island, the *ikomi* method is widely used.

Potter's wheels and molds developed differently in each region. These differences stemmed from the quality of clay available and from different regional customs. Molds give a set shape to ceramic ware and uniformity is possible if the same mold is used, but it is a very restrictive and static method of making shapes. Much skill is required to achieve a similar degree of uniformity with the potter's wheel, but free and unrestricted shapes are possible. When we see the variety of ceramics made, we can readily imagine the hard work of those nameless artisans who have made these fine objects since childhood. They had to undergo training in which they were not recognized as full-fledged potters until they could throw three hundred *domburi* a day on the wheel, shape the body of a *dobin*, and then put on its other parts accurately. Such training was the foundation on which the activity of the common people's kilns was based.

33. Haori: *Japanese coat. Deerskin; length, 95 cm. Nineteenth century. Tokyo. Japan Folk Crafts Museum, Tokyo.*

TEXTILES Textiles in Japan, as elsewhere, are characteristically used for clothing, including obi, kimono and its matching accessories, and also for making curtains, partitions, *noren* (door hangings), and *futon* (bedding quilts). Before synthetic fibers were invented, only natural fibers were used as raw material, and in Japan silk was the only fiber not obtained from plant sources. Bast fibers, which are inside the stalks and trunks of plants, were the most common kind of vegetable fiber, the types known as *asa* being the main ones. The use of these fibers for textiles goes back to ancient times.

Silk fiber is made from cocoons of both wild and cultivated silkworms. The qualities of each type differ, but after dyeing the colors of both have vividness and luster. Silk was such a valuable textile that sumptuary regulations were often made prohibiting its general use by the common people, and it was chiefly used to make ceremonial dress. Even now the word *kinu* (silk) is sometimes used to refer to kimono. Formerly the word referred to the outer skins of animals and plants, and then became restricted to mean the outer covering of the silkworm's chrysalis, i.e., the silk fibers of the cocoon. Except for districts specializing in silk production, silk was often woven mixed with cotton, and called *ito-ire* (cotton-silk weaving). *Ito* (thread) was another name for silk. Silk yarn comes in three forms: *ki-ito* (raw silk), *tama-ito* (thick, slubbed yarn taken

34. Karakusa-yaguji: *detail of material with arabesque design used for bedding. Cotton. Nineteenth century. Collection of Kichiemon Okamura, Tokyo.* ▷

36. Shibori: *Tie-dyed design. Silk. Nineteenth century. Narumi, Aichi Prefecture. Japan Folk Crafts Museum, Tokyo.*

◁ *35. Stencil-dyed continuous design on cotton. Nineteenth century. Kumano, Okayama Prefecture. Kurashiki Folk Crafts Museum, Okayama Prefecture.*

37. *Stencil-dyed* bin-gata *design on cotton. Seventeenth century. Shuri, Okinawa Prefecture. Collection of Keisuke Serisawa, Tokyo.*

38. Shibai-maku: *detail of stage curtain.* Asa. *Nineteenth century. Naha, Okinawa. Kumamoto International Folk Crafts Museum, Kumamoto Prefecture.*

39. Tejima: *hand-woven cotton-and-silk cloth. Nineteenth century. Shuri, Okinawa Prefecture. Japan Folk Crafts Museum, Tokyo.*

40. Tisaji: *handtowel.* Asa *and cotton; width, 25 cm. Nineteenth cen- ▷ tury. Yaeyama, Okinawa Prefecture. Japan Folk Crafts Museum, Tokyo.*

◁ *41.* Hishi-zashi maekake: *detail of apron quilted in a diamond design. Cotton and wool. Nineteenth century. Hachinohe area, Aomori Prefecture. Collection of Shoji Hamada, Tochigi Prefecture.*

42. Yaguji: *detail of material used for bedding. Cotton. Nineteenth century. Tottori Prefecture. Japan Folk Crafts Museum, Tokyo.*

from cocoons called *tama-mayu* containing two or occasionally three chrysalises), and *tsumugi* (a kind of homespun yarn made from the floss taken off the outer layer of cocoons, from imperfect cocoons, and from *tama-mayu*; this too is a thick, slubbed yarn). Of these, *tsumugi* has a particularly pleasing bulky quality.

The meaning of *asa* is ambiguous because it is used for a wide range of fibers. In a broad sense it stands for strong, stiff fibers cool to the touch that were first gathered in ancient times before plants were cultivated. The fibers of the *kozo* (paper mulberry), *kaji* and *shina* (types of mulberry), and wisteria are often called *asa* and made into textiles popularly known as *tafu*. Even the fibers of the *irakusa* and the *akaso* (plants of the nettle family) and those of banana leaves are sometimes called *asa*.

According to a narrower definition, the word includes flax, hemp, ramie, and jute. Hemp and ramie have been traditionally used in Japan. Hemp, a member of the mulberry family, does not grow wild but is cultivated, and ramie, a member of the nettle family, grows wild. Before cotton was discovered, any fiber other than silk was called *asa*, and cloth woven from these fibers was called *nuno* (cloth).

Although cotton wrinkles easily, it is softer, and people favored it over *asa*. Cotton has a relatively short history in Japan; its cultivation began after Hideyoshi's invasion of Korea in 1592–93. As cotton grows best in temperate climates, its cultivation in the northern part of this country was delayed. Cultivation was begun in Setouchi, the area about the Inland Sea, and then gradually

43. Stencil-dyed bin-gata *design on cotton. Seventeenth century. Shuri, Okinawa Prefecture. Collection of Toyotaro Tanaka, Tokyo.*

spread throughout the country. By the end of the Edo period, excluding the far north, yellow and white flowers of cotton plants were to be seen throughout the country. On level land suitable for the cultivation of cotton plants, *asa* was quickly superseded by cotton, and even people who lived in remote and secluded mountain areas or in the cold northern districts purchased cotton and wove it into cloth. The material was greatly welcomed by the common people, as we can see from the rapid growth in its popularity.

In addition to the foregoing, the fibers of *fuyo* (a type of rose mallow), *mitsumata* (daphne), *kuzu* (arrowroot), *zemmai* (flowering fern), the banana plant of Okinawa, the *adan* (a screw pine that grows near the shore on Okinawa), and the *yuna* (a flower resembling the hibiscus that grows near the shore on Okinawa) were used. The fibers of the rose mallow and the daphne are similar to those of the paper mulberry and *kaji*. Arrowroot was woven into *kamishimo* (a stiff kind of formal outer apparel) and into raincoats, which are the special products of Kakegawa in Shizuoka Prefecture. The fibers of the young buds of the flowering fern were used as a substitute for cotton, mainly in the northern part of Japan. The regions had to be self-sufficient with regard to textiles, and they therefore had to use whatever materials were at hand. As a result, textiles made in various parts of Japan had distinctive regional characteristics.

There are different methods of spinning fibers into yarn. Silk is drawn from cocoons, and *asa* and

44. Manzai-isho: *detail of material for a strolling comic dancer's costume. Asa. Sixteenth century. Aichi Prefecture. Japan Folk Crafts Museum, Tokyo.*

45. Kihachijo: *(literally, "yellow* hachijo*")* *predominantly yellow check-design. Silk. Nineteenth century. Hachijo Island, Tokyo. Japan Folk Crafts Museum, Tokyo.*

cotton are spun. The fibers are arranged parallel to one another and after the thicknesses are made uniform a twist is imparted. The yarn thus made can then be woven into cloth. All looms were hand looms until recently, and among the various kinds of hand looms there is an old type that is low in height called a *jibata* (ground loom). This loom is still used in Ibaragi Prefecture. When weaving with the *jibata,* the warp and weft become intertwined so that the characteristics of knitting remain, and the resulting cloth looks good and is comfortable to wear. Such material is more flexible and elastic than that woven on the *taka-bata* (high loom), where the warp is tightly held. Textiles are sometimes woven with undyed yarn, but in recent times, dyed yarn is generally used. Plain white cloth is used for mourning clothes, and *katabira,* a cloth made from

asa, has been traditionally used for this purpose. That this type of cloth continues to be used for funeral wear today shows how conservative human beings can be.

Natural dyestuffs are used to dye yarn, and in Japan only vegetable dyes were originally used. Red was made from safflower and madder. Yellow and the colors ranging from gray to brown have been very popular, and the main sources were the Myrica (aromatic shrubs and trees, wax myrtles or bayberries). Other commonly used dyes came from: *kariyasu* (a member of the rice family that gives a yellow dye), turmeric (a plant of the ginger family), plums, mountain lacquer trees, walnuts, *kunugi* (*Quercus serrata,* a kind of oak), gall nuts, sumac plants, and the black alder. The need for self-sufficiency led to regional differences in the making

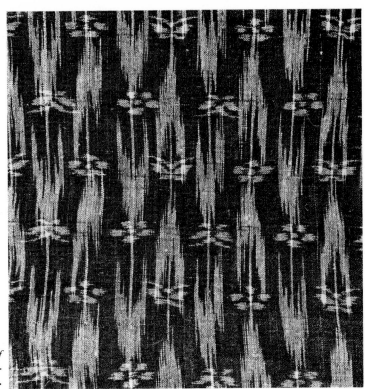

46. Geometric kasuri *design.* Chijimi *crepe of* asa. *Nineteenth century. Ojiya, Niigata Prefecture. Collection of Toyotaro Tanaka, Tokyo.*

and usage of dyes, as it did in the case of fibers. The *ki-zome* dye is made from *fukugi,* a bastard gentian found in Okinawa, the yellow dye used in *kihachijo* (yellow silk cloth made on Hachijo Island, Tokyo Prefecture) is from *kariyasu,* auburn is made from *inu-gusu,* (a type of camphor tree), black from *Pasania cuspidata* (a member of the beech family), the dark brown in Oshima *tsumugi* (a cloth made from *tsumugi* yarn on Oshima Island, Kagoshima Prefecture) comes from *sharimbai,* a kind of plum tree, and the brown in the *hachijo* of Akita (black, brown, and yellow patterned cloth) is made from the sweet brier. These dyes, along with the *shikon-zome* (deep purple dyes) of the Tohoku district, are all commonly used. Both the black of *hachijo* and the dark brown of Oshima *tsumugi* are produced by steeping yarn in mud with a high iron content. This process is called *doro-zome* (mud dyeing). In addition, imported dyes became popular: dyes from the *suo* (judas tree) are red; *tangara,* belonging to the mangrove family, produces a brown dye; and there were also dyes from the *binroji* (betel nut).

Dyes from the indigo plant were the most widely used. Its colors are roughly classified into *kamenozoki* (very light blue), *asagi* (light blue), *nando* (grayish blue), and *kon* (dark blue). The refined, clear, and fresh colors of indigo dyes have made them most highly valued. The plants from which the dyes are made belong to the smartweed family, so the dyes are also called *tade-ai* (smartweed indigo). The indigo dye used in Okinawa is called *kara-ai* (Chinese indigo). The red flowers of the indigo plant can be seen on patches of farmland throughout

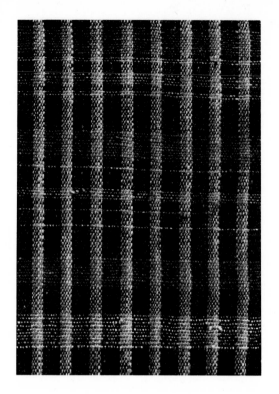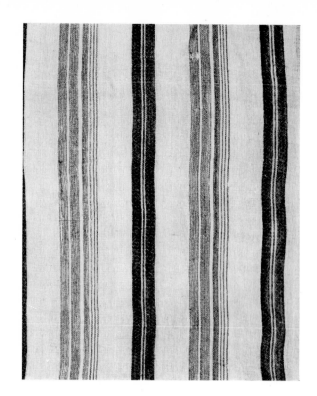

Japan, but they are cultivated especially in the district along the Yoshino River in Tokushima Prefecture, and it is here that *tama-ai* and *sukumo*, dyes made from fermented indigo leaves, are produced. These dyes are also called *awa-ai* (indigo from Awa, the former name of Tokushima Prefecture).

Dyed yarn is sometimes woven into a solid colored cloth, but people also enjoy cloth with a variety of colors. The weaving of stripes into a fabric is technically easy and can be done even in the simplest weave. This type of design is used throughout Japan. There are vertical stripes (Fig. 48), horizontal stripes, and checks; and stripes that vary according to color, the spacing between them, their width, and the quality, thickness, and texture of the yarn. Apart from the areas that make textiles as a special product, for example Hachijo, which

produces *kihachijo* (Fig. 45), striped cloth also came to be woven by the common people after the middle of the Edo period. Tamba cloth (Fig. 130), Mikawa (in Aichi Prefecture) cotton cloth, and that of the Shonai area in northwest Japan are representative materials. There are many cotton materials named after the districts in which they are produced, but there are even more striped cotton cloths that are not so named. Striped cotton material became the fabric of the common people, and there are few peoples who have such a variety of striped patterns as the Japanese.

Kasuri, a fabric of the chiné type, represents another way of patterning a plainweave fabric, and achieved a high level of development in Japan. The simplest method of making *kasuri* yarn is by binding skeins of yarn at certain points before dyeing. The bound sections do not take up the

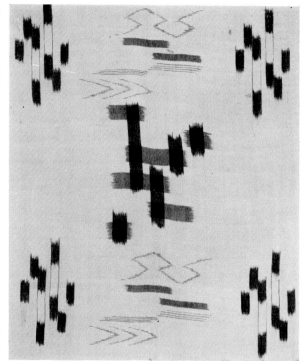

◁ *47 (opposite page, left).* Shima-ori: *detail of woven stripe design. Cotton. Nineteenth century. Niigata Prefecture. Collection of Kichiemon Okamura, Tokyo.*

◁ *48 (opposite page, right).* Shima-ori: *woven stripe design.* Asa. *Nineteenth century. Shuri, Okinawa Prefecture. Japan Folk Crafts Museum, Tokyo.*

49. Geometric kasuri *design.* Asa. *Eighteenth century. Yaeyama, Okinawa Prefecture. Japan Folk Crafts Museum, Tokyo.*

dye and thus retain the natural color of the yarn. Otherwise the sections to be left undyed can be compressed between boards (as in Shiga, Nara, and Ishikawa prefectures), or dyestuffs can be rubbed into the bundled yarn at certain points so that only those parts are colored (as in the Yaeyama group of the Ryukyu islands). *Kasuri* yarn can be used either for the warp, or the weft, or both, and it is often used in combination with plain yarns. When *kasuri* yarn is used for the warp, the warp threads are so arranged on the loom that the undyed parts form the desired pattern. Similarly, when the weft is interwoven with the warp, each weft thread is positioned so that the undyed parts build up the pattern. This "adjusted-weft" technique, in which each length of weft thread is carefully shifted by hand until the undyed part is in the right position, is termed *teyui*. The simplest

designs are star and cross shapes, and their irregular edges, due to slight "inaccuracies" in the positions of the undyed sections of the yarn, produce the streaky watered effect characteristic of *kasuri* (Figs. 39, 49, 50).

Kasuri techniques came from the Indonesian islands or China to Okinawa, later **developing** into the beautiful *teyui iro-gasuri* (multicolored *kasuri* made by the *teyui* method). From Okinawa it traveled north to Japan, where the geometric *kasuri* patterns, in part a development from stripes, were developed into *e-gasuri,* or picture *kasuri*. In one method of making *e-gasuri,* the weft is dyed in such a way that, when the cloth is woven, the undyed parts automatically come in the right positions for the design. This involves the use of a stencil, and preparation of the yarn for the weft is a long process, but designs of great intricacy are

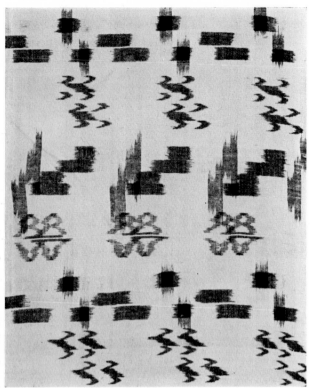

50. *Geometric* kasuri *design. Cotton. Nineteenth century. Shuri, Okinawa Prefecture. Japan Folk Crafts Museum, Tokyo.*

possible (Figs. 52, 59, 60). This new technique developed on the Japanese mainland made possible the creation of an amazing number of complicated representational designs. Many types of *kasuri,* each with its own characteristics, came to be made not only in areas which specialized in *kasuri* production, like Kurume (Fukuoka Prefecture, Kyushu) and Ehime Prefecture on the island of Shikoku, but also other areas like San'in (roughly that part of the Japan Sea coast along Shimane, Tottori, Hyogo, and Kyoto prefectures), Hokuriku (roughly that part of the Japan Sea coast along Fukui, Ishikawa, Toyama, and Niigata Prefectures), and the Kyoto, Nara, and Osaka area. It is interesting to note that the *kasuri* produced in Kurume, Ehime Prefecture, and the San'in area is of cotton, while that produced in the Kinai (Kyoto, Nara, and

Osaka) and Hokuriku areas is made from *asa.* The *kasuri* made in Ojiya, Niigata Prefecture (Fig. 46), is particularly famous. Most *kasuri* patterns are built up of the undyed parts of the yarn on an indigo ground, but Nara Prefecture is well known for its *shiro-gasuri* (literally, "white kasuri"), in which the ground is left undyed. In contrast to the famous *ikat* (a *kasuri*-type cloth from the area of the Indonesian islands), which is basically a fabric with the *kasuri* yarn in the warp, Japanese *e-gasuri* is basically a weft *kasuri.*

A vast variety of *kasuri* types is woven in Japan: white, indigo, multicolored; warp, weft, warp-and-weft; combinations with stripes; *teyui, e-gasuri,* etc. And there is no other country in the world where so many different methods are used and so many different designs created. *Kasuri,* with its

51. Noren: *decorative door curtain. Cotton; length, 50 cm. Nineteenth century. Collection of Toyotaro Tanaka, Tokyo.*

52. Kasuri-yaguji: *detail of e-gasuri (picture kasuri) material used for bedding. Cotton. Nineteenth century. Kannon-ji, Kagawa Prefecture. Kurashiki Folk Crafts Museum, Okayama Prefecture.*

53. Shikon-shibori: *purple tie-* ▷
dyed cotton. Nineteenth century. Hanawa, Akita Prefecture. Collection of Keisuke Serisawa, Tokyo.

54. Kogin: *white cotton quilting on base-cloth of indigo asa. Nineteenth century. Hirosaki area, Aomori Prefecture. Japan Folk Crafts Museum, Tokyo.*

55. Mino: *straw raincape. Length, 120 cm. Twentieth* ▷ *century. Tsugaru area, Aomori Prefecture. Japan Folk Crafts Museum, Tokyo.*

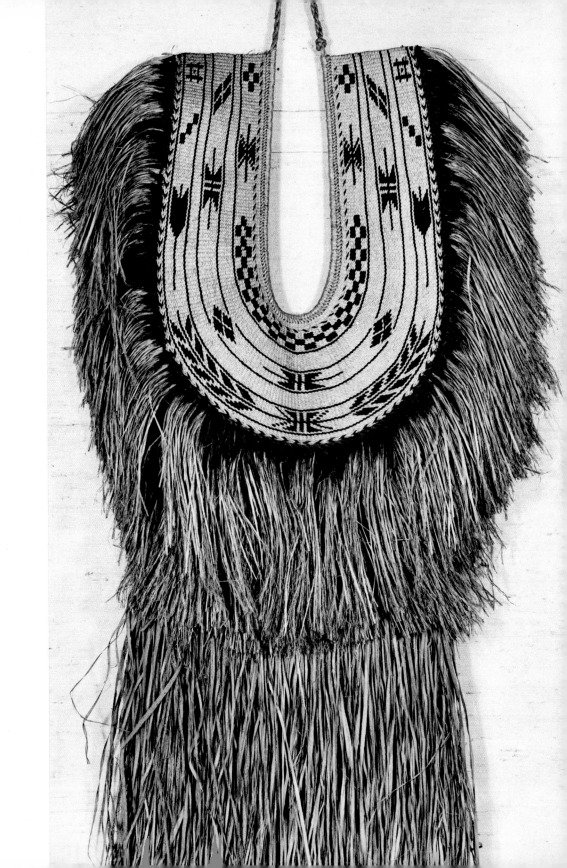

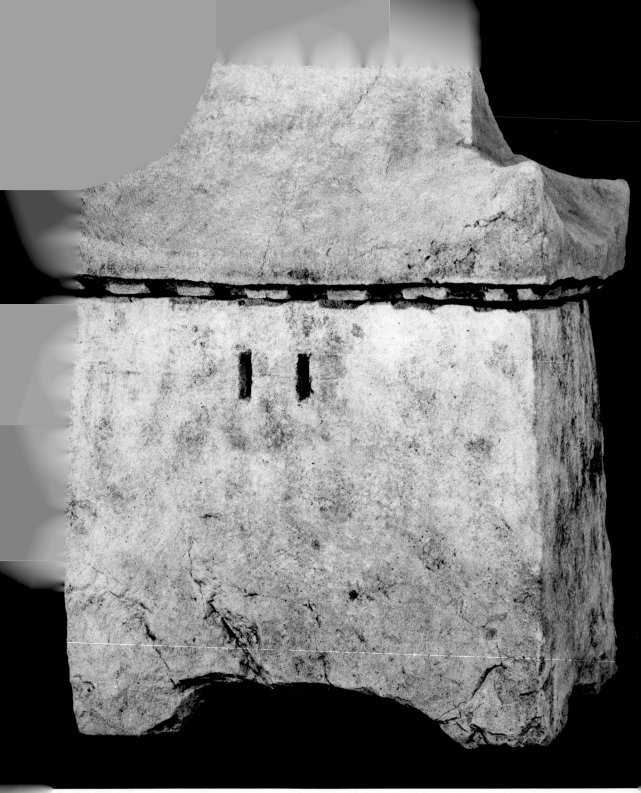

Zushi-game: funerary urn in the shape of a shrine. Coral; height, 63 cm. Seventeenth century. Yomitanzan, Okinawa Prefec-
Collection of Shoji Hamada, Tochigi Prefecture.

57. Arare-gama: (literally, "hail-stone pot"). Pot used for heating water. Iron; height, 22 cm. Nineteenth century. Iwate Prefecture. Japan Folk Crafts Museum, Tokyo.

58. Ema: *votive tablet. Colors on wood; 22 × 22.5 cm. Nineteenth century. Hachinohe area, Aomori Prefecture. Collection of Toyotaro Tanaka, Tokyo.*

59. E-gasuri: *detail of picture-*kasuri *design. Cotton. Nineteenth century. Ehime Prefecture. Collection of Kichie-mon Okamura, Tokyo.*

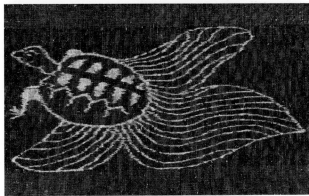

60. E-gasuri: *detail of picture-*kasuri *design. Cotton. Nineteenth century. Yumi-ga-hama, Tottori Prefecture. Japan Folk Crafts Museum, Tokyo.*

blurred and sheared effects, is without doubt an important inheritance of Japanese popular culture that must not be overlooked.

The types of cloth discussed above are all plain-weave, the simplest weave, in which each weft yarn goes over and under alternate warp yarns. More complicated fabrics are *aya-ori* (twill weaves) and *mon-ori* (figured weaves), of which the Okina-wan *hana-ori* (Fig. 100) is a simple example. The *tisaji* (Fig. 40), a handtowel traditionally presented by girls to their sweethearts, and the *minsa* (Fig. 147), a kind of narrow belt, are other examples of *hana-ori.*

A rather different kind of fabric, rare in Japan, is *dantsu,* hand-knotted rugs. Although the pile of rugs and carpets is generally made of wool in other parts of the world, Japan had no tradition of using wool and cotton was used instead. Representative types of *dantsu* are Nabeshima (made in Saga Prefecture, Kyushu; Fig. 128), Ako (made in Ako, Hyogo Prefecture), and Sakai (made in Osaka). The plainness of the people's lives was reflected in their not wasting clothing or fibers: *kuzuito-ori* were woven by utilizing left-over yarn, and *boro-ori* or *saki-ori* were materials woven by a method where the weft was made of rags of used clothing (Fig. 129).

From ancient times, it was the woman's duty to procure clothing for the family, so as well as learning how to cook, she was taught how to weave and sew. The sound of looms could be heard in villages throughout Japan, even in the most secluded places.

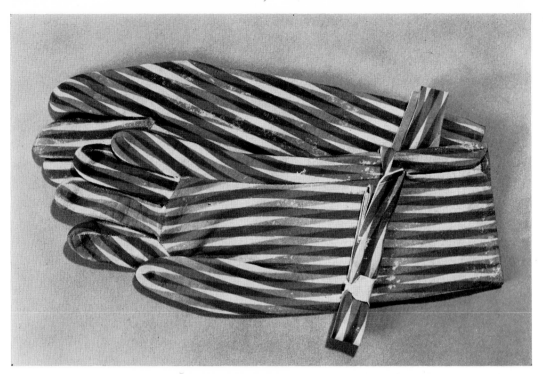

61. Tebukuro: *gloves. Deerskin; length, 32 cm. Nineteenth century. Tokyo. Japan Folk Crafts Museum, Tokyo.*

The weavers of the famous weaving districts were generally women, and although weaving was a source of pleasure for them, it also meant hard work that did not allow them to express their personal preferences. This can be seen in their *shimacho*, or pattern books, in which they carefully pasted woven samples for reference when weaving. Not only cloth that had been woven on their own looms, but any piece of cloth, no matter how small, was important. They took apart used account books, turned the pages over, rebound the book, and then pasted in their samples. These *shimacho* are very beautiful, and they are steeped in the fate of Japanese women. *Shimocho* demonstrate to us the deep roots of Japanese textiles.

Although the dyeing process is also used for dyeing cloth in one color, the methods to be considered here are used principally in applying de-signs to cloth. Because the Japanese people have a special interest in dyeing, there are unlimited numbers of patterns of birds, flowers, scenery, arabesques, and geometrical figures in bright and gay colors.

Traditional Japanese dyeing, called *wa-zome*, includes a number of techniques: *tegaki* (freehand designs); starch-resist dyeing (*nori-zome*), in which starch is used to cover the parts that will not be dyed; tie-dyeing techniques (including *ita-jime*, in which parts of the cloth are compressed between boards to prevent those parts being dyed); and blockprinting. Hand painting is done only on *noren* (curtains hung in the doorways of shops and private residences). A typical method is that used in Kyoto, in which the cloth is given a leatherlike stiffness by applying a kind of whitewash called *gofun*, after which the design is drawn with *sumi* ink.

62. Uma-no-haragake: *part of ornamental trappings for a horse. Cotton; 46 × 66 cm. Nineteenth century, Yamagata Prefecture. Collection of Takeshi Itsumi, Yamagata Prefecture.*

Resist-dyeing, which utilizes substances which prevent the cloth from taking up the dye, is a very common indirect method. Wax is a frequently used resist, but another method, highly developed in Japan, is the starch-resist method. This method uses a paste made from glutinous rice as a resist, and designs can be applied either freehand (*tsutsu-gaki,* using a tube from which the paste is squeezed out), or by means of a stencil (*kata-zome*).

Tsutsu-gaki allows the designer great freedom and is mainly used to apply large pictorial designs on things like curtains, banners (Fig. 13), *noren* (Fig. 51), festival costumes, bedding (Fig. 42), *furoshiki* (squares of cloth used for wrapping and carrying things), and horse trappings (Fig. 62). This pictorial type of textile decoration, by a combination of Japanese motifs with gentle colors, evolved into the subtle, painting-like designs of the *yuzen* textiles

developed in the Edo period. *Inaka-yuzen,* with its gradations of shading added with brushes, is an outstanding example.

The use of stencils allows the dyeing of more than one bolt of the same design, and moreover, stencils are suitable for making long continuous patterns (Figs. 35, 44). Designs not possible with the *tsutsugaki* method could be made. Arabesque designs (Figs. 34, 126) and small, delicate designs and stripes are representative of this method of dyeing. Because of an abundance of high quality glutinous rice and strong hand-made paper (from which the stencils are made), stencil dyeing developed and contributed to the spread of dyed textiles. There were dyers all over Japan—in every little country town, however small—supplying the local demand for stencil-dyed cloth. The town of Shiroko in Mie Prefecture specialized in the cutting

63. *Stencil-dyed* bin-gata *design on cotton. Nineteenth century. Shuri, Okinawa Prefecture. Collection of Keisuke Serisawa, Tokyo.*

64. *Stencil-dyed* bin-gata *design on* asa. *Nineteenth* ▷ *century. Shuri, Okinawa Prefecture. Collection of Keisuke Serisawa, Tokyo.*

of stencils, and these were so popular that there was virtually no part of Japan that did not have fabrics dyed with these stencils. Patterns numbered in the tens of thousands. The dyed materials produced by local dyers to fulfill regional demands are called *jizaiku* (local handwork). Such examples include the *tokiwa kon-gata* (dark blue indigo patterns) of Miyagi Prefecture, and though there is great variation depending on the region, the stenciled patterns (Fig. 6) found in the Shonai area (Yamagata Prefecture) are especially outstanding.

Among designs for which a paste-resist is used, the Okinawan *bin-gata* (in which red patterns predominate; Figs. 37, 43, 63, 64, 65) and the *ai-gata* (indigo patterns) are most noteworthy. Stencils are used to dye these patterns on kimono, while *tsutsugaki* is utilized in dyeing *furoshiki* (Fig. 12) and

curtains (Fig. 38). The dyed patterns stir our imaginations, like the clear, colorful picture scrolls of the southern islands that unfold island scenery in endless succession. In paste-resist dyeing, dyes and paints can be used together, and this method reached its zenith in the dyed cloth of Okinawa. *Bin-gata* and *ai-gata* are of the most beautiful colors, and the designs too are so superb that they cannot be further improved upon. Every possible technique has been tried in the field of stencil dyeing.

Tie-dyeing is an older method than *norizome*. The material is gathered in bunches or pleats, tied or sewn, then drawn up tightly to prevent penetration by the dyes. The wrinkles that naturally appear and the irregular shadings that result from the partial penetration of the dyes give the cloth a quiet and fresh beauty. The designs are not made

65. *Stencil-dyed* bin-gata *design on* asa. *Eighteenth century. Shuri, Okinawa Prefecture. Collection of Keisuke Serisawa, Tokyo.*

from set patterns. In starch-resist dyeing, the dyes are applied by brush, while in the tie-dyeing process the material itself is dipped into the dyes. Therefore the colors of tie-dyed cloth are much richer than those obtained by other techniques.

Depending on the method of tying, different patterns are made: *kanoko* (a number of round designs resembling an eye and its iris), *hitta* (similar to the *kanoko* design but square), *miura* and *boshi* (both similar to the two just mentioned, but with a slightly different use of the thread), *yoro* (vertical designs symbolizing a waterfall), *tazuna* (a chainlike design), *yanagi* (vertical designs symbolizing willow leaves), *moku* (vertical woodgrain designs), *tatsumaki* (large whirling designs), *kumo* (a spider-like design), *arashi* (meaning storm; this is a

large design with many fine lines), and others.

The major areas of production are Kyoto, known for its silk products, and Arimatsu and Narumi in Aichi Prefecture, known for their cotton products (Fig. 36). But because tie-dyeing can be done by almost anyone, great quantities of simply designed *shibori* have been made by Japanese housewives in various parts of the country. The *akane shibori,* in which red dye from plants of the madder family is used, and the *shikon shibori,* purple tie-dyed cloth (Fig. 53), both types made in Hanawa, Akita Prefecture, and the *beni shibori,* a red tie-dyed cloth made in Yamagata Prefecture, retain some of the ancient patterns.

Ita-jime is a resist-dyeing technique in which a design is carved on the surface of two wooden

66. Ita-jime: *a tie-dyed design obtained by compressing parts of the cloth between boards. Cotton. Nineteenth century. Kanazawa, Ishikawa Prefecture. Collection of Keisuke Serisawa, Tokyo.*

boards or blocks, and perforations are made in the boards. The cloth is placed between these blocks and tightly bound. Dye is then poured through the holes to color the open spaces, or the whole bundle is dipped into the dye. Materials dyed by this method have a beauty of blurred and diffused colors different from the previously mentioned *shibori*. For technical reasons, thin cloth is preferred for *ita-jime*, and *ita-jime* fabrics are widely used as lining material for kimono. At present *sekka shibori* (snowflake design) is probably the most common lining material. Materials for kimono worn in the home combine the techniques of *ita-jime* and *tsumami shibori*, in which the material is held in bunches by hand and dyed (Fig. 66).

Leather dyeing holds a special position of interest in the field of dyeing and is generally called *inden* (from the Portuguese *Indien;* Figs. 33, 61). Leather dyeing is associated with the traditional military equipment of the warrior class. *Shobu-gawa* (leather decorated with painted irises), *kozakura-gawa* (leather decorated with a cherry-blossom design), and *tombo-gawa* (leather with dragonflies) are all symbols of the samurai. Most leather goods were dyed by painting with brushes, but there is also *kusube-gawa*, or smoked leather. Its colors, though limited to yellow, brown, gray, and dark brown, are of soft and refined tones that harmonize very well with the leather. Dyed leather is divided into two categories: *inden* in its narrow definition, referring to the crests, stripes, and geometrical patterns for the dress clothes of lower-ranking samurai, the

67. Sashiko: *quilted coat. Cotton; length, 130 cm. Twentieth century. Noto area, Ishikawa Prefecture. Toyama City Folk Crafts Museum, Toyama Prefecture.*

style-conscious among the master-carpenters and firemen, and other commoners; and *uzura-gawa* (leather painted with quail designs), used for the hunting costumes of high-ranking samurai. At first leather was dyed in Edo (the former name of Tokyo), but later much leather dyeing was also done in Kofu, Yamanashi Prefecture.

As finishing processes, aside from dyeing there are appliqué, embroidery, and quilting. Appliqué designs are cut from cloth into the desired shapes and sewn onto clothing. The technique is often seen in crests and in designs for firemen's outfits. The Ainu, a people who inhabited the main island of Japan at one time but now live in Hokkaido, use appliqué designs extensively. Good examples of Ainu appliqué work are the *attush* (a warm, coat-like, short kimono made from bark fibers of the

elm; Fig. 98) and the *chikara karape* (a quilted and appliquéd short coat; Fig. 127), which have embroidery added to the appliqué. The spiral motif of the latter, influenced by the designs of the Jomon culture, which flourished in Japan up to about 200 B.C., has a strangely forceful appeal.

Embroidery is a purely decorative technique, but quilting aims at patching or strengthening and is a technique that developed inevitably from a simple way of life in which people could not waste cloth. Two types of design developed: pictorial and geometric. Quilting developed in connection with fishermen's clothing (Fig. 67), and in the Tohoku area (the northernmost part of Japan's main island, Honshu), with its long, cold winters. Representative are the *hishi-zashi* (quilting in diamond-shaped patterns; Fig. 41), made around Hachinohe (Ao-

68. Wan: *bowl. Lacquer over wood; height, 6.5 cm. Seventeenth century. Iwate Prefecture. Collection of Toyotaro Tanaka, Tokyo.*

69. Wan: *bowl. Lacquer over wood; height, 7 cm. Nineteenth century. Sendai, Miyagi Prefecture. Collection of Soshichiro Mori, Miyagi Prefecture.*

mori Prefecture), and *sashi-kogin* (Figs. 54, 99), quilting that was first made in about 1783 in the vicinity of Hirosaki (Aomori Prefecture) and in the Shonai area on the Japan Sea coast (Yamagata and Akita Prefectures). *Hishi-zashi* has white and dark blue threads running through the light blue cotton cloth, while *sashi-kogin*, with its white cotton stitchwork on dark blue *asa* cloth, gives an impression of snowflakes falling from the dark winter skies.

WOODWORK Japan—a long chain of islands running from north to south—is a mountainous country with a high humidity. Because it is rich in various types of plants, there is an abundance of materials for making wooden articles. It has coniferous trees such as pine, *sugi* and *ate* (Japanese cedars), Japanese cypress, fir, etc., and its broad-leaf trees include elm, paulownia, oak, and beech. These woods all have their own individual beauty: the straight grain of cedar, cypress, and paulownia; the fine grain of camphor and oak; the hardness of the intricately grained elm, cherry, and grapevine; the softness of the paulownia and the graceful flexibility of the willow; the oily sheen of the camellia and *ego-no-ki* (snowbell); the whiteness of paulownia; the yellow of mulberry; and the dark hues of ebony, rosewood, and black persimmon. Naturally, the choice of wood for a particular purpose depends not only on appearance but also on functional criteria. Desks and chests of drawers, for example, are surfaced with the hard woods elm and cherry, which have a beautiful grain, while paulownia, readily absorbing moisture and fire-resistant, is used for drawers.

70. Tebako: *box for keeping stationery, correspondence, and other small items. Lacquer over wood; 31 × 37.5 cm. Fifteenth century. Japan Folk Crafts Museum, Tokyo.*

The oldest types of wooden articles are those made of bark, and include such objects as pots, ladles, dishes, and other containers. Such articles have certain characteristics in common with leather products. The oldest articles of bark which continue to be made at present are those of birch. The beautiful bark of the wild cherry tree is popular and is used to cover cigarette cases, tea containers, and makeup boxes.

Mage-mono (literally, "bent things") is a technique that developed out of barkwork. Instead of bark, thin sheets of wood are bent into the required shapes (Fig. 71). Before saws came into use, the sheets were made by splitting wood with a billhook. The straight-grained conifers lent themselves to this method of splitting and so came to be extensively used for *mage-mono*. Light and resilient, they

are easy to carry and are used for things like ladles, lunch boxes, containers for cooked rice, and steaming trays. The method is used for making round and oval objects, as well as basically rectangular objects with rounded corners. A typical example of the latter is the *sambo*, a tray on a tall foot used for votive offerings. The most commonly seen *mage-mono* are frames for sieves. *Mage-mono* are also lacquered, and Shunkei lacquerware is a good example. Articles made from bent bamboo include the *mentsu* (a round container for cooked rice) and the traylike container called *hiro-buta*.

Hollowed-out articles (Figs. 8, 14, 135), easily made with cutting tools like the adze and chisel, are also examples of woodwork found early in history. Even now we can see such items as canoes, bailers, lipped bowls, kneading bowls, mortars (Fig.

71. Yuto: *warm-water pitcher. Lacquered wood; height, 23 cm. Nineteenth century. Onikobe, Miyagi Prefecture. Collection of Tomomori Okina, Miyagi Prefecture.*

122), tubs, *shamoji* (paddle-shaped rice servers), spoons, and wooden clogs. No old wooden articles have been excavated, since wood rots in the ground, but we know that they were important articles of everyday life. Primitive peoples who do not have pottery mainly use hollowed-out wooden vessels. Until recently, such articles were common in inaccessible mountain regions even in Japan.

Carved objects are used chiefly as decorations and include: pot hangers for use over open fires (Fig. 9), *ramma* (transoms between the ceiling and a lintel; Fig. 145), *kaeru mata* (wooden legs resembling a frog's legs, used as decorations between the ceiling and the *ramma*), and smaller articles, such as incense cases. Woodcarving is frequently used to decorate furniture.

Wooden articles are much stronger than earthen-ware, and most bowls and dishes were made of wood until the middle part of the Edo period. The appearance of the lathe brought an epoch-making change in wood-working techniques. This change was similar to that brought about by the introduction of the potter's wheel in ceramics. Whereas the potter's wheel rotates horizontally, the lathe rotates "vertically." Depending upon how the material is held, the wood may be cut across or along the grain. Articles manufactured by turning on a lathe are called *hikimono*, and the lathe made it easy to manufacture rounded objects, which up until then had been difficult, in quantities. *Hikimono* include trays, bowls, cylindrical objects, and incense containers (Fig. 121). By varying the circumference, various shapes are possible. In manufacturing articles such as the *heishi* (a bottle with a narrow mouth,

72. Choba-dansu: *chest for accounts and ledgers. Wood and iron; height, 90 cm. Nineteenth century.* Collection of Shoji Hamada, Tochigi Prefecture.

resembling a sakè decanter), the upper and lower parts are made separately and joined later. Articles turned on a lathe have a neater beauty, different from the rough, strong beauty of hollowed-out articles.

Joinery work is used in making *tansu* (chests, usually with drawers), paper-covered sliding doors, inkstone cases, and other types of boxes, *naga-hibachi* (rectangular braziers), ritual articles such as household shrines (Figs. 119, 120). The commonly used *tansu* and desks with sliding doors or drawers are structurally complex. There are great differences between Western-type furniture, which is centered on much standing and sitting on chairs, and Japanese furniture, for use in rooms where people sit on matted floors. In Edo-period furni-

ture, the greatest complexity and variety are exhibited by *tansu*. They are subdivided into dressers, *choba-dansu* (chests for accounts and ledgers; Fig. 72), *cho-dansu* (chests for notebooks and the like; Fig. 73), *zeni-dansu* (money chests), *kashi-dansu* (for cakes and candy), *kusuri-dansu* (for medicine), and *funa-dansu* (for use on ships; Figs. 7, 15). The names of chests of drawers are also determined by shape and size as for example the *yonshaku-dansu* (four-foot *tansu*), *ko-dansu* (small *tansu*), *kuruma-dansu* (*tansu* on wheels), and *kasane-dansu* (stacked *tansu*). *Tansu* have different designations according to the areas in which they are produced, and the dimensions used for *tansu* made in the Kanto area differ from those used in the Kansai area. Furniture such as chests of drawers, kitchen cabinets,

73. Cho-dansu: *chest for notebooks and the like. Wood and iron; height, 65 cm. Nineteenth century. Kurashiki Folk Crafts Museum, Okayama Prefecture.*

cupboards, and desks are called *sashimono* (cabinet work). Pieces like single-panel screens (Fig. 158) and armrests (Fig. 157), which consist mainly of flat areas rather than enclosed spaces, are called *itamono* (roughly, "boardwork"). *Itamono* give an impression of neat, orderly beauty. Japanese woodcraftsmen have established a worldwide reputation for their technical skill. Desks in which, when one drawer is pushed in, the resulting air pressure forces another drawer out, show an excellence of workmanship unparalleled in other countries of the world.

Casks, buckets, and tubs (Fig. 160) are another type of article made from boards. In this case, while the bottom is made from flat boards, the wall is made from curved boards set up side by side

vertically and kept in position by means of hoops passed round the outside of the wall. Woodwork involving the use of hoops, from bathtubs to knife handles and sheaths, is called *taga-mono* (hoopwork).

If the appearance of a wood is beautiful it may be used in the untreated state. Otherwise the surface may be made attractive by sanding and polishing. To prevent staining and to make the wood more durable, oil or astringent juice may be applied, or the surface may be hidden by coating with paint or lacquer. The use of glazes on ceramics is analogous to this. Lacquer (*urushi* in Japanese), the refined sap of lacquer trees, is a product of the Orient and is the most beautiful coating for wood, resistant to both acids and alkalis. The lacquer of

74. Heishi: *sakè container. Lacquer over wood; height, 22 cm. Fourteenth century. Collection of Shoji Hamada, Tochigi Prefecture.*

75. *Hidehira* wan: *bowl. Lacquer over wood; height, 9 cm.* ▷ *Sixteenth century. Shobo-ji, Iwate Prefecture. Collection of Seizo Sugawara, Iwate Prefecture.*

Southeast Asia is thick and black, while that of countries farther north is transparent and of good quality. As ceramic ware is representative of China, so lacquerware is of Japan. It is an interesting fact that lacquer does not dry unless there is humidity and the temperature is above a certain level. It dries most quickly during the rainy season and therefore is generally produced in areas of the Orient having a rainy season. Although there is a large variety of materials that are lacquered—wood, leather, paper, cloth, and pottery—wood is most commonly used, with the largest objects being buildings and various types of furniture, and the smaller articles including boxes, trays, *heishi* bottles, bowls, sakè cups, and combs. Many kinds of table ware are lacquered because they would quickly become dirty if left uncoated. Pottery-

making developed slowly in the Tohoku district, so that until recently lacquerware was commonly used on the table and for important rituals and ceremonies. In temples, strongholds of conservatism that preserve traditions, the eating utensils are mainly lacquerware. Next in importance among lacquered articles are bookcases and other boxes, portable medicine boxes, and household Buddhist altars and their accessories.

There are two ways of using the sap extracted from lacquer trees. One way, *nuritate* or *hananuri,* is to give the sap luster by mixing it with oil. In many cases, pigments such as vermilion, Indian red, or Chinese ink are added. The article is coated with this mixture and is left unpolished. In another method, *ro-iro* or *kijiro,* lacquer without oil is applied and the object is polished later.

In addition to plain lacquerware, there are various techniques for applying designs. The making of *taka-makie* (gold lacquer in relief) and *kin-makie* (gold lacquer work) require much time and great skill, but these objects lack simplicity in their beauty. Rather than these techniques using gold, it is colored-lacquer (*e-urushi*) designs that form the main tradition of Japanese lacquerware, and many beautiful works of this type are made. *E-urushi* has a longer history than *makie,* and its production increased rapidly after lacquerware became a part of the lives of the common people. Fine articles such as *heishi* bottles (Fig. 74), trays (Fig. 150), dishes, bowls (Figs. 68, 75, 134), sakè cups, boxes (Figs. 70, 114), and covered containers (Fig. 113), etc., remain. Because of the special viscous quality of lacquer, the lacquer-painted designs show irregu-

larities and impressions of the brush strokes remain. Although *e-urushi* lacquerware is at present made in every region, Kuchiki in Shiga Prefecture, Kuwana in Mie Prefecture, Yoshino in Ishikawa Prefecture, and Jobo-ji in Iwate Prefecture were the outstanding lacquerware producing areas.

Mitsuda-e (Fig. 133), at first sight hard to distinguish from *e-urushi,* are designs done with pigments dissolved in oil, to which oxidized lead has been added as a desiccant for the oil. In addition, there are many other types of decoration: *raden* (mother-of-pearl inlay), *rankaku* (eggshells set in lacquer; Fig. 160), *tsuishu* (engravings made through several coats of red lacquer to make patterns in relief), *tsuikin* (a Ryukyuan method where paint is thickened, kneaded, and pasted on), *chinkin* (inlaid gold lines), and *haku-e* (silver or tin foil with lacquer ap-

76. Jizai-gake: *hanger for pothook. Wood; height, 49 cm. Nineteenth century. Collection of Kanjiro Kawai, Kyoto.*

77 (below, left). Shoi-kago: *basket carried on the back. Cherry bark; height, 30 cm. Nineteenth century. Takayama, Gifu Prefecture. Japan Folk Crafts Museum, Tokyo.*

78 (below, right). Nata-zaya: *sheath for billhook. Cherry bark; height, 24 cm. Nineteenth century. Takayama, Gifu Prefecture. Collection of Kanjiro Kawai, Kyoto.*

79. Andon-zara: *plate placed under an oil lantern. Earthenware; diameter, 22 cm. Nineteenth century. Seto, Aichi Prefecture.*
Collection of Toyotaro Tanaka, Tokyo.

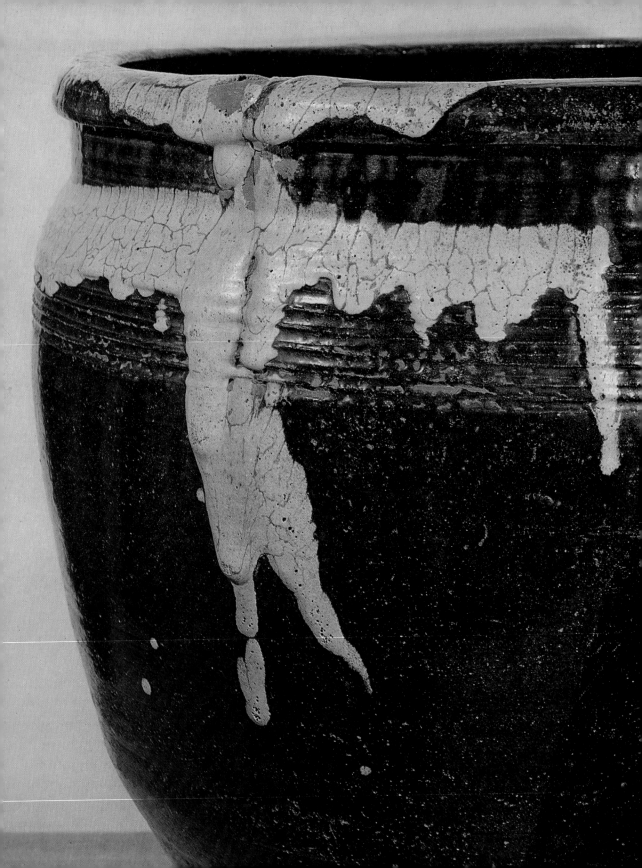

81. Mizu-game: *water-storage crock. Earthenware; height, 45 cm. Nineteenth century. Tsutsumi, Miyagi Prefecture. Collection of Sagoro Haga, Miyagi Prefecture.*

◁ 80. Mizu-game: *water-storage crock. Earthenware; height, 60 cm. Nineteenth century. Seiba, Nagano Prefecture. Matsumoto Folk Crafts Museum, Nagano Prefecture.*

82. O-zara: *large plate.
Porcelain; diameter, 44
cm. Seventeenth century.
Imari, Saga Prefecture. Ja-
pan Folk Crafts Museum,
Tokyo.*

83. Tokkuri: *sakè decanter. Earthenware; height, 19.5 cm. Nineteenth century. Tsuboya, Okinawa Prefecture. Kurashiki Folk Crafts Museum, Okayama Prefecture.*

84. Tokkuri: *sakè decanter.
Porcelain; height, 27 cm.
Seventeenth century. Imari,
Saga Prefecture. Collection of
Shoji Hamada, Tochigi Pre-
fecture.*

85. Sembei-tsubo: *crock for storing rice crackers.*
Earthenware; height, 50 cm. Eighteenth century.
Onda, Oita Prefecture. Japan Folk Crafts Museum, Tokyo.

86. *Basket for gathering bamboo shoots. Bamboo;*
height, 25.5 cm. Nineteenth century. Kyoto. Collection of Kanjiro Kawai, Kyoto.

plied over it). In *raden* and *rankaku*, the mother-of-pearl or eggshells are usually pasted randomly, not in regular patterns. The well-known *negoro* lacquerware produced at Negoro-ji in Wakayama Prefecture, was originally made by applying lacquer containing a ferric substance over which a vermilion lacquer was later coated. This technique is called *hananuri* (floral coating). As the vermilion lacquer becomes worn after long use, the black lacquer underneath is partially revealed. Such lacquerware differs from the modern version, where the black is deliberately brought out by polishing.

Basketwork and similar plaited articles exhibit one of man's oldest techniques. Although other techniques exhibit some changes after tens of thousands of years, in this archetype of technology the same methods are still being used. Moreover, plaiting is so universal an art that there is virtually no people, no matter how primitive its state, that does not practice it. The materials used in the process include practically every fibrous material conceivable: bamboo, vines, grasses, bark, wood, cloth, and even hair. The products of this process have a wide field of application, being used for dwellings, ships, fishing gear, floor coverings, containers, cooking utensils, and clothing and personal adornment. Basketry made from bamboo has a conspicuous role in Japanese everyday life. Basketmakers can be found in every town. There are many kinds of baskets (Figs. 86, 144, 155) for household, farming, and fishing use, such as *zaru* (a kind of sieve), *soke* (a shallow bamboo sieve used in the Kansai district), wastebaskets, *midare kato* (a

88. Bunko: box for keeping stationery, correspondence, and other small items. Bamboo grass; height, 14 cm. Twentieth century. Nagano Prefecture. Matsumoto Folk Crafts Museum, Nagano Prefecture.

87 (left). Mino: raincape of shuro (hemp-palm) fiber. Length, 120 cm. Twentieth century. Miyazaki Prefecture. Matsumoto Folk Crafts Museum, Nagano Prefecture.

basket to hold one's clothes when taking a bath), flower baskets, fish baskets, etc. Bamboo is used to make screens, umbrellas, hats, lantern frames, brush holders, and ladles. *Madake* (the most common type of bamboo, having long joints) is used most widely, followed by *mosochiku* (a species of bamboo originally from China). In northern areas of Japan, where bamboo does not grow, *shino-dake* (bamboo grass; Fig. 88) is used. Among bamboo-plaited products for special uses, there is the *miki-guchi*, plaited bamboo used to decorate sakè bottles placed in household altars at New Year's. The *miki-guchi*, decorated with pasted red and gold paper, has a neat, fresh beauty.

Mino (straw raincoats; Figs. 55, 87) are indispensable for working in the mountains or fields. The best *mino* are made in the northern part of Japan. *Mino* come in many shapes and are made chiefly of straw, but also of sedge, pampas grass, bulrush, rush, lime bark, the bark of the Japanese cypress, nettle, hemp palm, and seaweed. For their best wear the villagers used colored threads and edged the hems with cloth to add color. Patterns were woven into the fabric of the *mino* and great care was taken with their shapes. These were called *date-gera* or *iwai-gera* and were men's presents to women. *Se-ate*, used to protect the back when carrying wood (also called *bandori*; Figs. 123, 124), vary in shape and in the type of plaiting used. The *se-ate* of the Shonai area are considered the best. There are many styles used in the plaiting of headgear, and the *obana-boshi* (hat with a floral tail) used by hunters is very unusual. Articles necessary for working in the mountains and fields

89. Tetsubin: *kettle. Iron: height, 14 cm. Eighteenth century. Tottori Folk Crafts Museum, Tottori Prefecture.*

include *nata-zaya* (billhook sheaths; Fig. 78), *shoi-kago* (baskets carried on the back, also called *ko-dashi;* Fig. 77), snowshoes, straw sandals, straw slippers, and gloves. Besides these there are round straw cushions, various types of mats, hampers, brooms, pot rests, noodle scoops, etc. Braiding and plaiting are very basic handwork techniques, and it is this characteristic that is the source of their beauty. Too neat materials and techniques result in delicacy. And this is not desirable, for the beauty of plaiting derives from a strong, sturdy vigor.

METALWORK Gold and silver are used mainly for ornaments such as bracelets, rings, earrings, *kanzashi* (ornamental hairpins), and combs, while copper and iron are used chiefly for articles of practical use. Although iron rusts, it is abundant, and takes on different characteristics when carbon and other metals are added. By applying pressure or heat, iron can be hardened or annealed, and it is often cast and forged.

Broadly speaking, the processing of metals is divided into casting and forging. In the casting process, metal is melted at a high temperature, poured into molds, and then cooled and hardened. The resulting article is called a casting. Products include iron kettles (Fig. 89), *kama* (iron pots; Figs. 57, 159), pans, *mizugame* (water containers), *hibachi* (braziers), steamers, trivets, lanterns (Fig. 136), and *rogane* (pothooks suspended over an open hearth). Casting is also used for Buddhist and other sculptures. In one method of making molds, a model of the object to be cast is first made from wood (sometimes wax). The model is buried in

90. Osome-jo: *a type of storehouse lock. Iron; width, 15 cm. Twentieth century. Kochi Prefecture. Japan Folk Crafts Museum, Tokyo.*

sand, and then removed in such a way that the hole left in the sand keeps the required shape. Molten metal is then poured into this mold. The metal flows in with great force and rapidly solidifies. The violence of the casting process and the hardness of the material both contribute to the powerful shapes of cast wares.

In forging, iron is shaped by hammering in a hot state. Forged iron is denser in structure, and more malleable and resilient than cast iron. Typical forged products are: knives, adzes, planes, saws, gimlets, and scissors. Swordmaking achieved a high level of development in Japan, and its techniques were later applied to the manufacture of farm implements. Every town or village had its smiths making sickles, plowshares, hoes, billhooks, and knives, as well as locks (Fig. 90), pothooks, etc.,

many of which had special regional characteristics. Billhooks, especially, came in various shapes and sizes.

Alloys, mixtures of two or more metals, are a special feature of metalwork. Bronze, an alloy of copper, tin, zinc, lead, and other metals, is used even today in making statues, and because of the pleasing sound it makes when struck, it is used for percussion instruments such as temple and other bells, gongs, etc. Brass, an alloy of copper and zinc, is tensile and comparatively rust-resistant. And because it has a pleasing luster like that of gold, it is widely used in articles for Buddhist altar fittings. Articles made of brass include candleholders (Fig. 137), locks, fire irons, ash levelers used with *hibachi*, flower vases, portable brush-and-ink cases, and tobacco pipes (Fig. 91).

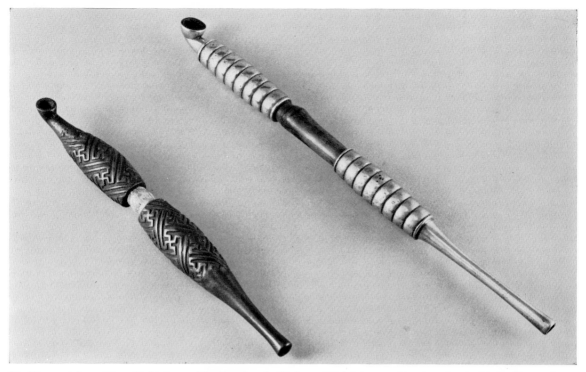

91. Kiseru: *tobacco pipes. (Left) iron and bamboo; length, 22.5 cm. (Right) brass and bamboo; length, 31 cm. Nineteenth century. Collection of Kanjiro Kawai, Kyoto.*

Objects used for reinforcement purposes, such as metal fittings, clasps, and hinges, utilize the inherent strength of metals. These beautify and strengthen buildings, furniture, boxes, and clothing accessories. Methods of decorating metalwork include engraving the design on the mold (in the case of castings), *sukashi-bori* (openwork), *ke-bori* (hairline engraving), where the carving is done with a burin, and *zogan* (inlay), where thin strips of gold, silver, copper, brass, tin, etc., are tapped into grooves. This technique is frequently used for small ornaments. Metal foil is very tensile and is ideal for use in gilding, *kiri-gane* (designs made up of pieces of gold and silver foil), and *haku-oshi* (foil pressed onto the surface of an article). It can also be powdered and sprinkled on as decoration. Foil is used for a great variety of applications.

FOLK PICTURES Pictures were originally religious accessories, and thus, since they had a nonartistic purpose, were a form of applied art. *Minga* (folk pictures) are examples of such applied-art pictures. Based on a number of simple techniques, they include genres like *hanga* (woodblock prints), *ema* (literally, "picture horses"; votive paintings, originally of horses), *otsu-e* (a genre using a medium of pigments mixed with clay, lacquer, and ash), *doro-e* (a genre using opaque pigments), *garasu-e* (paintings on glass), traditional battledore (*hagoita*) decorations, and *karuta* (pictures on cards used in a poem-guessing game). *Minga* is an art form strongly bound by conventions not only in technique, but also in size, purpose, subject matter, and pigments.

Woodblocks are used to print paper amulets and

92. Ema: *votive tablet. Colors on wood; 12 × 15.5 cm. Nineteenth century. Kofuku-ji, Nara Prefecture. Japan Folk Crafts Museum, Tokyo.*

kisho-gami (vows of religious faith), trademarks, wrapping paper, *chiyo-gami* (decorated paper used for making paper dolls, small boxes, etc.), maps, articles used in games, and book illustrations. Sometimes colors are added by hand or with stencils.

The votive tablets called *ema* (usually of wood; Figs. 58, 92), used as offerings to shrines and temples, are examples of hand-painted folk pictures. These tablets originated in the custom of making offerings of live horses to shrines and temples, and so representations of horses were common at first. However, the subject matter rapidly came to include the animals of the zodiac, pigeons, foxes, eagles, parts of the body, and even objects that were being prayed for. *Ema* display regional differences, and the place of origin can be told by their subject matter, shape, thickness, and size. The Nara and Tohoku regions have produced many fine *ema*.

The battledores called *hagoita* resemble *ema*, but their decorations are even simpler.

Otsu-e (Figs. 10, 131) are included among the souvenirs of Kyoto that were sold by the roadside at Oiwake on the Otsu Highway in Shiga Prefecture about the middle of the Edo period. At first Buddhist subjects were represented, but subsequently secular subjects and subjects from popular religion also appeared. Old *otsu-e* were rather small and were in the so-called *kaki-byoso* format. This is a kind of "false mounting" painted around the picture proper so as to suggest the cloth borders used in mounting pictures as hanging scrolls (Fig. 10). Sizes gradually increased but eventually returned to the original small format. The treatment is simple, and methods used include woodblocks, paper stencils, compasses, and templets. The colors available were very restricted, and were used skillfully to achieve the colorful effects of *otsu-e*.

93. Doro-e: *painting in opaque colors on paper; 46.5 × 36 cm. Nineteenth century. Nagasaki. Japan Folk Crafts Museum, Tokyo.*

94. Doro-e: *painting in opaque colors on paper; 26 × 40 cm. Nineteenth century. Nagasaki. Collection of Toyotaro Tanaka, Tokyo.*

The name *doro-e* (mud pictures) derives from the fact that these pictures were painted with opaque pigments. The interesting point about them is that perspective was employed. Beginning in the middle of the Edo period, there were the Nagasaki *doro-e* (Figs. 93, 94, 132), those of the Kamigata (Kyoto) area, and those of Edo. The *doro-e* of the Nagasaki style are the oldest and quite colorful, and because they included pictures of foreign customs, Dutch-style mansions, ports, and ships, an exotic atmosphere was created. The Kamigata-style paintings frequently show famous places of Nara and Kyoto, and, though colorful, they create a quiet impression. Pictures of the Edo style, which developed last, used indigo almost exclusively, and frequently depicted famous places in Edo, which indicates that the pictures were meant as souvenirs of Edo. Small *doro-e* were used in peep shows. Edo *doro-e* have a conspicuously stereotyped style due to conventionalized draftsmanship.

Pictures were also painted on the back of glass sheets. This was a difficult method because right and left had to be reversed, and the last stroke had to be done first. Glass painting in Japan started in Nagasaki and was introduced from Europe via China. The greatest number of glass paintings was produced in Edo, and they were mainly of genre subjects.

CHAPTER THREE

The Appreciation of Folk Crafts

ARTS AND CRAFTS show the relationship between people and utensils in the way these utensils are used, made, and appreciated. Because these relationships are so closely linked, it is impossible to consider them separately. Before taking a utensil into our hands to use it, we always look at it. This is necessary to locate it and to ascertain its shape and size. Decisions concerning its beauty cannot be made without seeing it. Since seeing is that which belongs to the senses, we are accustomed to letting objects capture our attention at random in our ordinary experience. In this case, an explanatory association of ideas emanating from many years of experience is naturally included. For example, suppose there is a tea bowl on a table. The table has a flat surface with legs under it, and sometimes it has drawers. We can recognize the tea bowl by its size and shape, and we can also judge its colors and quality. Such aspects of concrete things, learned from past experiences, are stored in the brain as knowledge and concepts. This is an extremely general way of viewing things in our ordinary, day-to-day life—that is, an objective view. The other way of viewing is the subjective view. Just as the words indicate, it is based on individual experiences centering on oneself, and there is an additional tendency toward more sensuous appreciation. Whether using an objective or subjective view, one must take into account the person who is looking, the utensil being looked at, and the general concept that relates them. Using either viewpoint singly leads us to view things on the basis of no more than a general knowledge, so we carelessly make random judgments without noticing distinctive features. Such a general view involves unnecessary, extraneous concepts, so that the viewer is said to be "seeing without looking."

FROM INTUITION TO INTELLECT

To say that there is a subjective view and an objective view means that there is a view without conceptualization at all. It is an important view that simply senses beauty without concepts—that is, by intuition. For example, there are times when one experiences an exultant impulse at the instant one sees an article, and from that point on, there is continued pleasure in having seen something of value. The unexplainable surprise, the joy and purity that arise from coming close to the core of beauty, soothes the human mind and stimulates the development of the human spirit. Intuition is a spontaneous feeling and a spontaneous way of looking at things, but afterwards intelligence takes the role of systematizing these impressions. The true nature of intuition is not something abstract; on the contrary, it is a concrete emotion deep enough to create a physical reaction. This pronounced tangibility forces one to understand by experiencing beauty directly, not by reasoning about it. Where there is intellection there is always dualism, because the intellect always divides. Thus, through intuition, one can take ex-

terior phenomena and integrate them at the very foundation of one's mind, at a place deeper than one does with reasoned knowledge and sensation.

It is human nature to pursue knowledge in its every aspect. Human nature shows interest in everything and longs to know. This peculiarity has enabled human civilization to progress. The nobility of human beings is manifested in this very tendency to be dissatisfied when even the smallest and obscurest matter has not received its share of attention. Such an attitude leads to the systematization of these problems into knowledge and the discovery of the direction toward understanding. In order to formulate one's ideas intellectually it is necessary to arrange things at definite points in the system. This in turn necessitates one's taking a fixed view of things. The same objects can be classified into different categories leading to different ways of seeing, feeling, and thinking. These various stances, in turn, allow different means of expression.

Intuition can be expressed only by an exclamation of wonder, but appreciation changes with the particular utensil being studied, the times, and the persons involved. That attitudes toward objects thus change means that different viewpoints are defensible. The same object can be appreciated from different approaches.

THE THING AP-PROACH AND THE FACT APPROACH Starting with the simplicity of intuition, the pattern of what I call the "thing" approach is to cherish the beauty of an object, enjoy an emotional experience from it, appreciate it and thereby deepen one's experience of life. This approach stresses the primacy of beauty: beauty is everything. The special characteristic of those adhering to this approach is that they fully value their own intuition and have an immutable, special love for beautiful things. Having personally experienced beauty, they are

97. Tsubo: *crock. Earthenware; height, 26.5 cm. Eighteenth century. Naeshirogawa, Kagoshima Prefecture. Japan Folk Crafts Museum, Tokyo.*

motivated to treasure beautiful objects, and it is because they love these articles that they are capable of this intuitive sense.

On the other hand, one's intellectual, not intuitive, understanding is suitable for explaining to or convincing others. Who used the article? What was it used for? Where was it produced? In what era was it produced? All of these facts become important. Instead of the article itself, the circumstances take precedence. This is the "fact" approach. When a person looks at a utensil and asks: "I wonder what it is? What can it be used for? What is it called?" then he is "fact" oriented. If instead he uses words like "beautiful," "pretty," "amazing," and "overwhelming," then he is "thing" oriented.

Thing-oriented people, not bothering to build a framework of facts, instantly take an arbitrary position, but fact-oriented people take time to order their observations. By observing how people look at a utensil, it can be said that human attitudes can be broadly divided into the rational and the emotional. But one cannot make a sharp distinction between these two because each individual has both within himself. It is undoubtedly true that there are few people without an appreciation for beauty, nor are there many lacking a desire for knowledge. It is more a matter of a difference in degree. Even the person who assigns more importance to beauty also has a desire to obtain knowledge.

Both feelings and intellect are based on facts. Pure intuition is simply the immediate transformation of facts into knowledge. It is possible to proceed from pure intuition to the construction, the putting together, of concepts, but not vice versa. If one meddles with concepts first, one cannot even perceive beauty. By starting with concepts, one is already working within a framework of a definite position which limits one's perception. Pure intuition has fundamental value in that emotion deep

98. Attush: *short, coat-like kimono made from elm-bark fiber. Length, 114 cm. Nineteenth century. Hokkaido. Collection of Keisuke Serisawa, Tokyo.*

enough to cause one to perspire from the pain proceeds to ideas that make clear the very source of beauty. Although it is extremely important to be deeply moved by beauty, simple agitation of feeling does not allow real appreciation of the object. In the consideration of beauty, feelings should always come first, with the use of the intellect following. It is the function of the intellect to transform the passive impression into an active thought.

THE VALUE OF PURE INTUITION Pure intuition springs from colorless, formless impulses and provides the basis of all that shapes each person's individuality. Tied in with daily life, intuition molds our ideas. There is no opinion as strong as one formed through intui-

tion. And there are few things that make life more pleasant than intuition does, as, for example, when one examines beautiful objects with the aim of using them. That there are many beautiful artifacts found among the ancient arts and crafts used by ordinary people is due to the work of the intellect to systematize as concepts what has been acquired through pure intuition. But not all folk-art objects are beautiful. One key point is that while there is no article that is considered unsightly, the judgment as to whether each one is beautiful or not can only be accomplished by independent intuition each time. It would be truly wonderful if one could conclude that all folk-art objects were beautiful, but one cannot come to such a conclusion because the folk artists themselves have human failings. To say that all folk wares are beautiful and

99. Kogin: *white cotton quilting on base-cloth of indigo asa. Nineteenth century. Hirosaki area, Aomori Prefecture. Japan Folk Crafts Museum, Tokyo.*

therefore good is no different from the type of thinking that credits the applied arts of the nobles with a particularly superior kind of beauty.

Through pure intuition we can find quite a number of objects outside the field of folk art that have a kind of beauty similar to that of folk articles. This may be illustrated by the Hidehira *wan* (Fig. 75). These black lacquer bowls decorated with red lacquer patterns and scattered goldleaf flecks are produced in the Tohoku area of northern Honshu. They were named after Fujiwara no Hidehira (?–1187), an early Kamakura-period (1185–1336) warrior. Another example is that of early Kutani *aka-e* ware, polychrome chinaware that was produced in Kutani, Ishikawa Prefecture. *Aka-e* ware contain a red coloring that was first used during the Edo period (1603–1868) in woodblock printing

(Figs. 11, 24). Other non-folk-art objects include dyed and woven materials such as *tsuji-ga-hana*, a tie-dyed material that originated in Kitsuji, Nara Prefecture, in which the tied portion was wrapped in bamboo bark and oil paper. In addition there were woven materials colored by the *yuzen* dyeing process. *Yuzen* was named after the painter Miyazaki Yuzen (1681–1763) of Kyoto. Dyers were said to have made imitations of his painted designs. By applying a specially prepared paste to prevent blurring during the dyeing process, they produced a cloth dyed in many colors. This method of stencil-dyeing gay colors and designs was unique to Japan. Kaga *yuzen*, unlike Kyoto *yuzen*, is dyed with a special plum juice produced in Kaga, present Ishikawa Prefecture. *Kobin-gata* is a traditional dyed material of the Ryukyu Islands whose pat-

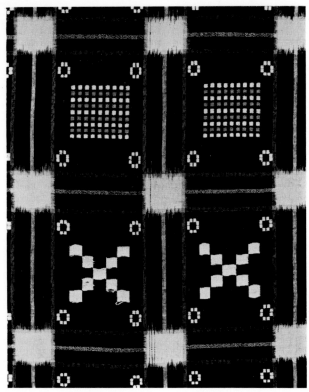

100. *Combined* kasuri *and* hana-ori *(a kind of tapestry weave) design. Cotton. Nineteenth century. Yomitanzan, Okinawa Prefecture. Japan Folk Crafts Museum, Tokyo.*

terns are made with stencils and various colors on cotton materials. Its special characteristics are its original designs and bright colors (Figs. 37, 43, 63, 64, 65). Okinawa's traditional *kasuri* is a form of woven material with varicolored thread that produces a splash pattern (Figs. 49, 50, 100).

There are many more objects that exist from the days before folk art achieved recognition, and a vast number of these primitive artifacts have been dug out of ancient graves. These articles show clearly that the "thing" approach is necessary, that intuitive appreciation of beauty is necessary.

It is impossible to understand folk art by just mouthing the word *mingei*. Efforts to recognize folk art did not begin only after the invention of this word. Many folk-art objects had existed prior to the terms and the word *mingei* came later to define the more outstanding articles. We should always keep in mind the fact that folk objects reflect the everyday life of ordinary people, and if the word *mingei* is defined in lofty and profound concepts, then this definition will misrepresent the true nature of the folk articles.

CHAPTER FOUR

Characteristics of Folk Crafts

THE GREAT MAJORITY of recognized folk-craft objects date from the middle of the eighteenth century to about 1868, although these articles were also used later, during the Meiji and Taisho eras. Articles of daily use were fated to be thrown away or buried and therefore there are no articles surviving from an earlier period. Japan was an isolated country during the Edo period, and it enjoyed a long age of peace. The people were rather poor, but the content of their lives became enriched, and a large variety of household utensils were made and carefully preserved. Under the feudal system, it was standard procedure for each daimyo to control his own territory. Goods were produced independently, and there were thus many distinctive varieties of regional folk crafts. These were carefully nurtured, and the folk-craft tradition grew more and more vigorous. Accordingly, many folk-craft articles still exist from this period. Yet only a few people showed interest in these objects and appreciated them for their aesthetic qualities. Folk articles began as things to be regarded in a matter-of-fact way and not as objects of beauty to be speculated upon. The beauty of any particular plate can be appreciated only by really examining it. Yet, no matter how detailed one's understanding of the making of the plate and of its function and its meaning to society both economically and historically, one is not assured of recognizing its beauty. Beauty does not originate from matters like these alone. The fact that one can grasp things intuitively means seeing their beauty, and it is after seeing that one can know truth. Knowledge that is not backed by intuition is empty.

Thus if one feels the beauty of a particular vessel, the fact of seeing it as something both beautiful and useful already means that it has intrinsic unity. It does not mean that one thinks about its physical function. It is as though the vessel has become one with the people who made it, looked at it, and used it. That is to say, it is being examined as an integrated form before emotion and objectivity become separated. At this point one must speak of the vessel as being a "body" inseparable from and bound to the human heart. Designs in which use and beauty are joined together are placed under the heading of applied arts. What features must there be if the people's arts and crafts are to be called applied-art articles?

PRACTICAL USEFULNESS
The basic attribute of folk craft is utility; the objects have practical value. In order for something to be useful in enriching daily life, it must not contain the superfluous or have a complicated form that cannot stand constant use. Decorative lines and complex designs that have no function are useless. The qualities of both utility and beauty are inseparably tied together in folk craft so that beauty apart from usefulness has no meaning. A folk object's beauty must lie in the realization of its use. The usefulness of an object increases if the shape

and design are suitable to its use, and if the objects are useful, they become even more meaningful.

But this does not mean that folk-craft objects are of practical use only. They must also fulfill the need for pleasing, comforting, purifying, and elevating the human spirit. Any departure from these needs would imply that the applied arts cannot exist. Folk crafts are related to the daily material and spiritual needs of the common people. Folk crafts are not determined by individual preferences and tastes, nor should they be determined by the arbitrary opinions of a few specialists. Folk crafts depend upon the wisdom of the masses and upon the directions their daily lives take. Folk crafts are based on a commonly shared way of life, on a background of long tradition and historical development that have conditioned the feelings and purposes of daily life. For this reason, folk crafts clearly, simply, and naively express the structure of society and the feelings of the people.

Artifacts that belong to the category of everyday usage are very different from decorative articles, and were long looked down upon as clumsy utilitarian objects. Still, because they fulfilled utilitarian needs, they were freed from the concept of beauty for beauty's sake, and more liberal ideas of beauty developed. In this way, usefulness became a necessary characteristic of the applied arts, and here beauty was determined by whether or not an object was useful.

LARGE QUANTITIES Mass production enables folk crafts to flourish. Objects must be produced in large quantities if they are to fulfill the needs of the people. In the art of dyeing there are stencils; in the art of pottery-making, form and patterns are determined by the potter's wheel; cast-metal articles are produced in quantity by using molds. Artistic skills acquire momentum from mass production. Methods of pro-

103. Chatsubo: *jar for storing tea. Earthenware; height, 13 cm. Nineteenth century. Tsuboya, Okinawa. Japan Folk Crafts Museum, Tokyo.*

104. Chatsubo: *jar for storing tea. Earthenware; height 38.5 cm. Nineteenth century.* ▷
Shigaraki, Shiga Prefecture. Kurashiki Folk Crafts Museum, Okayama Prefecture.

105. Ishi-zara: *stone-glazed plate.
Diameter, 36 cm. Nineteenth century.
Seto, Aichi Prefecture. Japan Folk
Crafts Museum, Tokyo.*

106. O-zara: *large plate. Earthenware; diameter, 35 cm. Nineteenth century. Shodai, Kumamoto Prefecture. Japan Folk Crafts Museum, Tokyo.*

107. O-zara: *large plate. Earthenware ; diameter, 34.5 cm. Eighteenth century. Seto, Aichi Prefecture. Collection of Shoji Hamada,*
Tochigi Prefecture.

◁ *108*. Tokkuri: *sakè decanter. Porcelain; height, 23.5 cm. Eighteenth century. Imari, Saga Prefecture. Japan Folk Crafts Museum, Tokyo.*

110. Yunomi: *tea bowl. Porcelain; height, 5 cm. Eighteenth century. Imari, Saga Prefecture. Tottori Folk Crafts Museum, Tottori Prefecture.*

109. Yunomi: *tea bowl. Porcelain; height, 5 cm. Eighteenth century. Hasami, Nagasaki Prefecture. Collection of Toyotaro Tanaka, Tokyo.*

duction become simpler and easier. Production is speeded up, and excessive technique and waste from the use of unnecessary materials are avoided. But as things are produced in large quantities, articles lose their individuality and are looked down upon as being very ordinary. Nevertheless, the needs of the public must be served. The beauty of folk crafts lies in the fact that there is nothing novel about folk articles. They are just average, ordinary, and widely used in the daily lives of the common people.

In mass production, a division of labor is necessary. Folk articles, whether made on a small or large scale, were in many cases dependent on a cooperative industry based on a division of labor. Prior to this, some craft products for private use were made from beginning to end by the same person. Cotton for private use was cultivated, gathered, dyed, and woven by a member of the

household and then made into wearing apparel for another member of the family. This was a local custom of long tradition. Spurred on by the need to produce standardized objects in large quantities, the production of an article came to be divided among a number of workers. This division raised manufacturing efficiency, and was carried out not only on a large scale in factory production but also on a smaller scale in cottage industries. In the production of lacquerware there were craftsmen who made the wooden base, those who painted on the layers of lacquer, those who painted the design, and possibly a specialist to apply the gold lacquer. Pottery production depended upon a division of labor among such workers as those who prepared the clay, used the potter's wheel, applied the glaze, did the art work, and fired the kiln. This breakdown made it possible to achieve mass production.

111. Ko-bachi: *small bowl. Earthenware; height, 6 cm. Twentieth century. Ryumonji, Kagoshima Prefecture. Collection of Shoji Hamada, Tochigi Prefecture.*

112. Kaku-bin: *square bottle. Porcelain; height, 20.3 cm. Nineteenth century. Imari, Saga Prefecture. Japan Folk Crafts Museum, Tokyo.* ▷

A folk-craft article completed from beginning to end by the same individual became a rarity and it was at this point that folk articles lost their identification with individual makers, and a signature that purported to be the maker's became meaningless.

LOW PRICES Because they were produced in quantity, folk-craft articles were low-priced. It was not only essential to produce them in large numbers for the populace, but the articles also had to be made available at prices low enough to be easily obtainable. Mass production made this possible. Before the economy came to be based on currency, objects used by individuals were either homemade or supplied by a cooperative system of production within one's group. Living needs were met by exchanging goods with other groups or households. But when the value of objects came to be expressed in currency, and money became essential for one's livelihood, it became necessary to establish prices within the monetary limits of the general public. In order to provide moderately priced articles, the cost of production had to be lowered by eliminating wastefulness. Therefore, the special characteristics of simplicity and wholesomeness inevitably developed in the folk crafts. At the same time, inexpensive production of these objects improved the quality of folk articles, and the basic attitudes concerning what

113. Futamono: *container with lid. Lacquer over wood; diameter, 13.8 cm. Eighteenth century. Collection of Toyotaro Tanaka, Tokyo.*

folk crafts should essentially be

When the original folk-craft objects were first being produced and used, the idea of low pricing had very positive effects. On the other hand, though, the combination of low prices and high production for commercial reasons had a negative and even a destructive effect on the folk crafts. Desire for profit led to a disregard of both utilitarian and aesthetic values and lowered the quality of an article and cheapened it. Commercial institutions played a large role in this process. From the first, folk products were naturally different from the individually made articles that concentrated on eye-catching beauty. The maker probably could decide the price of his products, but the low prices and rationalization of folk-craft manufacture should be were also formed.

determined as much as possible by the people who purchase and use the articles, as this preserves the essential character of folk crafts. Folk crafts lose their very nature if commercialism takes over. Cheaply made objects that ignore the true qualities of folk craft no longer belong to this category of articles.

REGIONALISM One essential element in the making of folk articles is the types of materials used. These materials are those that come from natural resources. Since Japan is a long, narrow chain of islands running from north to south, with rich geographic and climatic diversity, it enjoys a great variety of natural resources. Differences in climate and geography created a variety of life styles in which distinctive customs were nur-

114. Tebako: *box for keeping stationery, correspondence, and other small items. Lacquer over wood; 20.3 × 18.5 cm. Nineteenth century. Collection of Toyotaro Tanaka, Tokyo.*

tured, and daily necessities to accommodate these various ways of living were made from the natural materials found in the differing localities. Furthermore, during the Edo period each fief had to rely on itself for the production and supply of goods. Highly developed skills were kept within each feudal territory and not made known to those outside the fief. This greatly encouraged the development and the preservation of skills by region. The people of each fief, living under various restrictions within a feudal system that tied them firmly to their lands, were blessed with natural resources. Using these resources, they learned to make various utensils for their daily lives. In this way there developed an abundance of folk-craft products colored by regionalism. Even today, folk articles rich

in regional distinctiveness continue to be made. The artisans in the cities, separated from the land and cut off from nature, responded to popular demand. In the articles they made, they readily turned toward using complex techniques and away from functional, practical shapes. In comparison, most of the artisans outside the cities were in direct contact with the soil, and they were, therefore, strongly tied to nature and continued to preserve the original concept of the folk crafts.

THE ARTISANS   The production of folk articles was carried out not just by a handful of artistic geniuses but by a large number of ordinary craftsmen. For this reason, regional distinctiveness is said to be one characteristic of

115. Kasuri being woven. Hirokawa, Fukuoka Prefecture.

116. Dyeing yarn in vats. Hirokawa, Fukuoka Prefecture.

folk crafts. In general, the artisans did not express strong personal creativity and individuality. This was not because they lacked these traits, but because each occupational category worshiped its particular god and lived by the traditional skills passed down by its ancestors. Thus their traditions originated, so to speak, in cooperation with their ancestors. This tradition was the wisdom and experience accumulated over long years. It taught them that by working in harmony with and respecting nature, they could derive benefit. On the whole, superior folk crafts were made in areas and eras where the people were deeply religious. Such high-quality crafts were gifts granted in response to this religious spirit. The crafts depended upon that which transcended the individual, rather than upon the personal powers of the artisans who made them. Traditions changed with the times but the secrets of these skills, selected and improved, were passed down with family industries from generation to generation. The individual artisan was aided by this tradition of craftsmanship and by a deep belief in the tradition. The artisan also had the ability to accept easily that which nature had to offer. He was further helped by co-workers, both in the city and in the countryside, who guarded and refined the various techniques.

An artist is inspired by his emotions and absorbed into the act of creating. By nature he dislikes being restricted by that which is outside the self. It may appear that an artist may always do as he pleases, but producing a great number of goods within agreed-upon time limits for the daily life of the masses made it impossible for him to have his own way. They were not well off financially, so most of the artisans depended upon their skill and hard work in making folk-craft wares. The craftsmen were not necessarily happy all the time, but it cannot be denied that through their hard and trying labors, superb folk-craft objects emerged. As long as folk objects are limited to those made by hand, techniques developed from long years of skilled practice are necessary, and the skills involved must be mastered through repetition and hard work. The mastery of these skills and the urgency of the work brought about the simplifica-

117. Throwing on a Japanese potter's wheel. Mashiko, Tochigi Prefecture.

tion of the finished product and enabled the artisans to lose themselves in their work. Their labors resulted in products that showed a lack of consciousness of ego and had qualities of strength and simplicity. Very few of the artisans realized the significance of these rewards, but when their strenuous labors were over, the happiness and satisfaction they felt toward the completed folk articles were absorbed into and became part of the objects. The artisans were thus able to carry out their work in making folk crafts with the help of nature and tradition.

The early artisans did not sign the utensils they made, so that the lack of a signature is one of the characteristics of folk crafts. One reason they did not was that during some periods, except for artisans who had special permission, the authorities would not permit them to sign their wares. A more

118. Kyusu: *serving teapot. Earthenware; height, 8.5 cm. Eighteenth century. Tsuboya, Okinawa Prefecture. Kumamoto International Folk Crafts Museum, Kumamoto Prefecture.*

fundamental reason was that the low-cost production of a large quantity of goods made it essential to save time. Furthermore, the articles were from the first made not by one person but by the cooperative efforts of a large number of workers; and finally, the articles were unsigned because the workers did not have a strong sense of individuality or highly developed egos that would have led to their signing them. Utensils in which an artisan's individuality and ego were not reflected made it possible for the masses to feel relaxed, and thus they could depend upon these utensils in their day-to-day living. That their users could relax gives positive meaning to unsigned folk articles.

CHAPTER FIVE

The Beauty of Folk Crafts

THE MAIN CHARACTERISTIC of folk articles is their usefulness. One can sense the beauty of folk crafts by seeing utensils in actual use. When they are successfully fulfilling needs and are therefore showing their true character, they are very beautiful. The beauty of folk articles, then, springs from their usefulness in daily life—that is, beauty in service. In other words, use is the main characteristic of the utensils that carry out their functions and this is their true nature. How, then, does the true character of a utensil used as a folk article come into being, and what qualities of beauty appear?

Generally speaking, things have an intrinsic beauty, and are sufficient unto themselves. The real nature of beauty lies in the very impressions we receive of its freedom from all obstacles. The beauty of nature presents an extremely simple and pure manifestation of this essential characteristic of beauty. Therefore one can say that beauty is the manifestation of freedom; it is freedom that establishes the form. When utensils conformed to these natural laws, they became truly beautiful for the first time, and it was now possible for them to become folk articles. Materials that come from natural surroundings maintain the folk crafts: the craftsmen loved nature; they set a high value on natural forces and created folk articles in cooperation with it. Accordingly, the products were not contrary to the laws of nature, and they contained a natural beauty that arose spontaneously from within rather than from some abstract conception

of art. Nowadays, it is possible to notice many counterfeit articles that are called folk craft but which must be reclassified by the standards I have just mentioned. Today, most of us are estranged from nature because we regard it as something to be conquered. It is unfortunate that most useful articles for the common people no longer retain the same natural beauty that the folk crafts originally had.

As I mentioned earlier, the value of folk-craft articles lies not just in their appearance. Because folk articles must serve the needs of many people in their daily lives, they have to endure heavy use. These utensils ought to be designated as "bodies" in which the feelings of those who use them and those who make them are joined. To be useful, to be able to work, a body must be healthy. This does not simply mean that the flesh (clay) must be free of illness, for the heart must also be pure and free from worry or pain. If the materials are chosen for their utility and the utensils are made with earnest intent in accordance with the natural qualities of these materials, the resulting products will not be of a bizarre or inappropriate shape that obstructs their usefulness. A sick, weak, nervous body cannot bear up under use. That is why utensils that were created by the arduous labors of healthy artisans had a healthy beauty, a beauty both honest and genuine. Another characteristic of the beauty of folk crafts, then, is a wholesome, energetic beauty.

In the process of eliminating the wasteful in

order to mass produce products to be sold at low prices, none of the essential qualities of the folk objects were destroyed. Simplification means neither less content nor omitting a part of the essential nature of an object. Simplification is the crystallization of its essence. It involves the focusing of the essential into that which is highly concentrated. Things are made stronger, not weaker, through simplification, and one can sense a greater intensity of beauty if the object is simple. And because it has been simplified, a utensil can exhibit its real character more clearly.

The simplicity and plainness of the shapes of objects show humility and modesty of feeling. It is possible to read the mind that made and pursued these qualities as mind and matter are united in the utensils. Folk crafts, with their intrinsic qualities of simplicity and plainness, are in accordance with nature. Simplicity is the fundamental characteristic of beauty in folk articles. In contrast, elaborate and detailed techniques produce that which is just for diversion. Such objects are full of ostentation, extravagance, and haughtiness. These latter characterize the beauty found in the artistic applied arts of the nobility.

Folk articles are not strongly individualistic; instead, they are simple and they harmonize well in the lives of ordinary people. They can convey a sense of familiarity and a feeling of repose. And although there are various kinds of folk articles and each has its special charm, their appeal does not stem from the ego and individuality of the maker but depends instead upon the times in which they were made and the prevailing conditions of

119 (opposite page, left). Zushi: miniature shrine. Lacquered wood; height, 40 cm. Nineteenth century. Kurashiki Folk Crafts Museum, Okayama Prefecture.

120 (opposite page, right). Zushi: miniature shrine. Wood; height, 11 cm. Nineteenth century. Collection of Toyotaro Tanaka, Tokyo.

121. Kogo: incense container. Lacquered wood; height, 14 cm. Sixteenth century. Japan Folk Crafts Museum, Tokyo.

nature. Because folk-craft products are deeply rooted in nature, are created with its support, and are in tune with its ever-changing conditions, we find new and different types of articles being created one after the other, each with its own charm. In this process nature manifests itself through the medium of human beings, resulting in many stylistic variations, each with its own distinctive features. In the northern areas of Japan, much pottery had an earthenware body, but in the Seto area (near Nagoya) and in Arita (in Kyushu) hard wares having porcelaneous bodies were made. In places where cotton could not be grown, and until it became easy to acquire, it was necessary to use cloth made from *asa* for protection from the cold. There was no sense of inconvenience, as this situation was accepted as natural.

The main characteristic of folk articles is that they give a feeling of closeness and familiarity. If folk articles are made so that there appear struggles for self-expression and attention to unique characteristics, they are a burden and worry to those who use them. The beauty of folk crafts does not reflect ego-striving; it is selfless. This does not signify a loss of individuality and ego but the overcoming of a narrow and headstrong personality and ego that insist upon expression of their own will, to reach a true individuality that realizes its universal nature. A feeling of familiarity with the articles, meaning the unity of inner feelings with these objects, comes about if the objects express universal qualities. As the utensils become familiar objects to their users, their value increases and they take on even more beauty. The phrases "to become

122. Usu: *mortar. Wood; height, 49.5 cm. Nineteenth century. Gifu Prefecture. Toyama City Folk Crafts Museum, Toyama Prefecture.*

123 *(opposite page, left).* Se-ate: *back protector ▷ used when carrying firewood. Length, 120 cm. Twentieth century. Shonai area, Yamagata Prefecture. Japan Folk Crafts Museum, Tokyo.*

124 *(opposite page, right).* Se-ate: *back protector ▷ used when carrying firewood. Length, 88 cm. Twentieth century. Shonai area, Yamagata Prefecture. Chido Museum, Yamagata Prefecture.*

skillful in using" and "to become used to handling" mean that, because of the appreciation of the charm, the warmth, and the "softness" that these familiar articles possess, the articles have true meaning for the first time.

Up to now, we have talked about the various kinds of beauty of folk-craft ware, but now we must clarify the fundamentals that unite the various forms. When all is said and done, the beauty of the folk crafts is essentially an unadorned beauty. And because it is unadorned beauty, it is an ordinary beauty—one can even call it a free beauty.

The beauty of folk artifacts is deeply related to the daily lives of the people. The geniuses who sought after supremely beautiful things were unable to discover the meaning and true value of ordinary, plain things. Is it the ordinary and plain things that truly express beauty? Or do uncommon and rare things do so? If one evaluates beauty according to its grandeur or mediocrity, the end result is that one becomes bogged down in a contrast of beauty with ugliness. If the intellect becomes involved, one thing is pitted against the other and opposition results. Opposition is self-restriction, not independence and freedom. But, when we enter the sphere in which tranquillity represents nobility, and normal mentality represents the "Great Way," then nonbeing is no longer in conflict with being and the normal no longer simply negates the erratic. Tranquillity and normal mentality define an imperfect boundary that transcends the opposing forces of being and nonbeing and of the normal and the exceptional, and transcends that which distinguishes knowledge and ignorance. This sphere is

the abode of nature in its gentleness, and is where tranquillity and normalcy have risen above all contrivances. All things manifest a freedom in this spiritual world of nondistinction. Thus, beauty is not in conflict with ugliness. Until they are made separate, beauty and ugliness constitute a unity. This unity is nothing other than tranquil beauty. The discovery that the unity of tranquil beauty is of the highest kind, and the discovery that this beauty is a part of the folk crafts, was made by Soetsu Yanagi.

The artisans who made folk-craft wares did not have much knowledge to boast of. They did not have an intellectual understanding of this beauty and its principles. Neither did they depend upon themselves for their creations, but were much influenced by nature and tradition. In a way that is difficult to understand, they were able to make various articles of great beauty. Although the artisans did not have an individualistic tenacity of purpose, it cannot be said that they displayed absolute selflessness. And notwithstanding the fact that their religious obedience, based on tradition and nature, also influenced their work, they deliberately overcame willfulness by participating in the natural processes of nature. Thus adapting themselves to a tranquil beauty, they became the beneficiaries of these outside forces. Soetsu Yanagi's insight into special and hidden meanings came after reading the fourth vow of the forty-eight great vows of the *Daimuryoju-kyo* (Great Sutra of Infinite Life), which states: "I will not attain the state of enlightenment until I perceive a lack of distinction between good and evil."

CHAPTER SIX

A Brief History
of Japanese Folk Crafts

As EACH PERSON has a family name and ancestry, each vocation has a history or a process of creation or development. In this history there are always fluctuations owing to various causes and circumstances. In the art of weaving, for example, we find different types of materials being used, such as silk and cotton, with the development of each one proceeding differently. When one thinks about the applied arts as a whole, a complex of historical and technical elements and objectives is intertwined. This complexity does not have as its primary cause the extensive contacts between ordinary people and these arts, but its chief source is instead the diversified ways of life of the people. Folk crafts are one of the elements of civilized life created by the needs of living. Consequently, in the history of these crafts one recognizes many social factors. Examination of these factors by dividing the subject of folk crafts into several categories and examining them from various angles will allow us to understand the range and depth of the products that serve as the core of handicrafts.

The earliest applied-art objects are those made in the prehistoric era. It is often said that culture began with the use of magic, and the applied arts are no exception. It may be that it is an exaggeration to apply the term "applied arts" to the various kinds of wooden clubs and stone carvings of the

prehistoric age, but I believe that the applied arts were born about the time the small-scale community units led by chiefs and female shamans had begun to flourish to a certain degree. It would be helpful if one imagined oneself back at the beginning of the Jomon period (?–200 B.C.). The development of the intellectual powers of these primitive people was not advanced, in that they believed themselves moved by a force greater and stronger than any human being. They lived in a world of magic, trying to influence this force to their own benefit.

Even if magic is far more immature than religion, these people were moved by the greater power of nature, by a spirit that could not be denied. And it is possible to say that, although the people were wholly passive, artifacts that were distinctly human came forth from their hands. And because the people prayed out of fright and because fear was the main element in their lives, the earliest crafts had a sacred character. One can say that at this time all things were in a chaotic state. But chaos is different from confusion, and so a natural condition prevailed.

We cannot make a distinction between civilization and culture here: this is a special characteristic of prehistoric times. But within the narrow bounds of human existence clear distinctions along ethnic

125. Katakuchi: *lipped bowl. Lacquered wood; height, 18.5 cm. Eighteenth century. Collection of Shoji Hamada, Tochigi Prefecture.*

and regional lines arose as a matter of course. And when we consider that the prehistoric arts were influenced by magic, we cannot in our speculations ignore that force. Since the skills of the early craftsmen were primitive, the beauty of their arts was the result of doggedly persistent work over long hours which had as its source a strong and intense inspiration supported by magic.

As magic became more complex, remarkable decorations appeared on artifacts. These decorations appeared before the practice of distinguishing articles for ritual use, although it was not long before articles for daily use, those that had little decoration, were separated from the ritual articles, which had vivid, conspicuous decorations. Some earthenware of the Jomon period shows no traces of having been fired, and there are other artifacts of this time that are too small to have been of practical

use. This indicates that artifacts had already been separated into two distinct categories, those for ritual use and those for everyday use. Folk articles developed from these prehistoric objects, but despite this, it is clear that prehistoric artifacts cannot be classified as folk-craft articles. Archaeology has shown that the first prehistoric handicrafts were stone implements, followed by clay artifacts. By using stone cutting-implements, prehistoric men created objects of bark and wood, and made woven goods.

The replacement of stone tools by metal tools, the invention of the potter's wheel and the lathe, the development of high-fired ceramics, and the appearance of textiles are all developments of the arts that burgeoned in the ancient period. In the background, we sense that religion, developed out of magic with the aid of ratiocination, now governed

126. Karakusa-yaguji: *detail of material with arabesque design used for bedding. Cotton. Twentieth century. Collection of Kichiemon Okamura, Tokyo.*

men's hearts, and that a foundation of learning and thought had been established. One special feature of this period was the establishment of a system of rank based on heredity and occupation, which spurred the development of more advanced techniques for making objects. Although the development of the applied arts was determined by the rulers and upper-class families, objects for daily use continued to have the character of folk articles. Despite great interest in the kinds of folk articles that existed during this ancient period, regrettably little data are available because no such articles have been found among the artifacts excavated from the grave mounds of the ancient period.

Once the separation of ruler and ruled had taken place, this distinction appeared in artifacts also. There were no great differences between articles for everyday use and those used in rituals during the prehistoric age. But differences between, on the one hand, articles for the common people's everyday use and on the other hand, ritual objects and objects used by the ruling families and the nobility to display their power gradually became more pronounced. The ornamentation of the applied arts

of the nobility gradually came to have a technical independence and a recreational rather than a practical function. Many of these objects are beautiful. Techniques were being improved upon and experiments were constantly being made with new types of artifacts. Sharp-edged metal tools were developed, and cutting and shaving tools made possible detailed carvings that had been difficult up until then. There was a feeling of freshness stemming from a pioneering spirit that fostered beauty. This work was different in nature from the aristocratic applied arts of a later age. The appearance of ugliness was due to a stagnation of the pioneering spirit and to ostentatious self-consciousness. In these developments is to be seen the beginning of the transition from the ancient to the medieval period (approximately from the thirteenth to the sixteenth century).

Everyday articles of the ancient period are not in existence today because of their high rate of wear. Furthermore, the masses, divided into social classes, were more oppressed than they had been earlier, and with their freedom severely restricted, articles available for their use were probably less plentiful.

127. Chikara karape: *short Ainu coat with appliqué design. Cotton; length, 123 cm. Nineteenth century. Hokkaido. Collection of Keisuke Serisawa, Tokyo.*

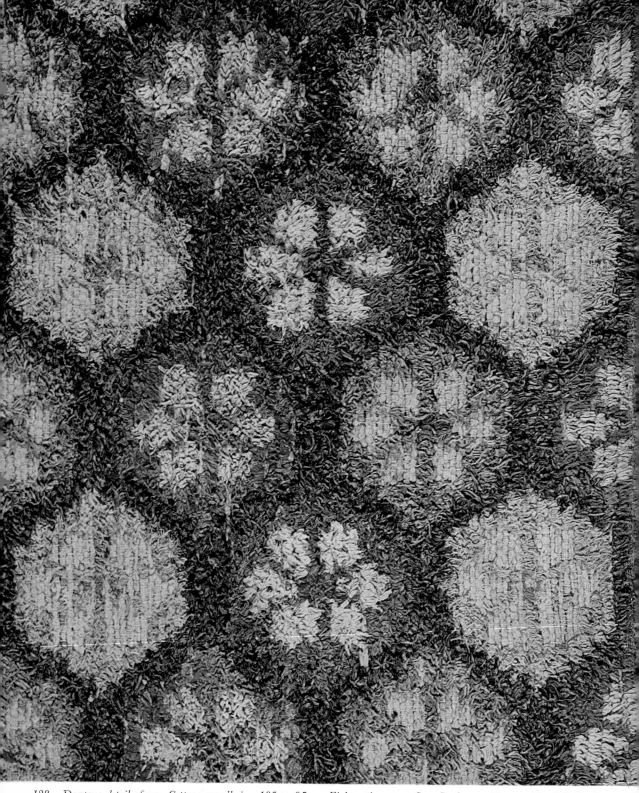

128. Dantsu: *detail of rug. Cotton; overall size, 185 × 95 cm. Eighteenth century. Saga Prefecture. Toyama City Folk Crafts Museum, Toyama Prefecture.*

129. Saki-ori: *material woven from old cloth. Cotton and silk; width, 30 cm. Eighteenth century. Japan Folk Crafts Museum, Tokyo.* ▷

130. Kaya: *detail of mosquito net. Cotton. Eighteenth century. Hyogo Prefecture. Japan Folk Crafts Museum, Tokyo.*

131. Otsu-e: *painting of a falcon. Colors on paper; 59.5 × 22.5 cm. Seventeenth century. Otsu, Shiga Prefecture. Collection of Masako Shirasu, Tokyo.*

133. Tebako-buta: *lid of box used for keeping stationery, correspondence, and other small items. Litharge colors on wood; 32 × 23* cm. Seventeenth century. Collection of Toyotaro Tanaka, Tokyo.

◁ 132. Doro-e: *painting in opaque colors on paper; 26.5 × 21.5 cm. Eight-eenth century. Nagasaki Prefecture. Japan Folk Crafts Museum, Tokyo.*

134. Wan: *bowl. Lacquered wood; height, 8 cm. Seventeenth century. Iwate Prefecture. Collection of Toyotaro Tanaka, Tokyo.*

135. Hachi: *underside of bowl. Wood; maximum diameter, 20 cm. Nineteenth century. Hokkaido. Japan Folk Crafts Museum, Tokyo.*

In the middle ages, which includes the Kamakura period (1185–1336), the Muromachi period (1336–1568), and the Momoyama period (1568–1603), the people continued to live in extreme poverty until finally their resentment exploded in insurrections and riots. It was during the middle ages that the ordinary people gradually displaced the nobility in importance. When meaningless ostentation, the disappearance of self-determination, and the ugly qualities of human nature became characteristic of the applied arts of the declining nobility, a separation of the applied arts of the people and that of the nobility took place. The objects of the nobility continued to change and become more refined, delicate, and estranged from practical use in daily life. *Tsuji-ga-hana,* Hidehira *wan* bowls, *bin-gata* stencil dyeing, and the *kasuri* of Okinawa are examples of articles for the daily use of the nobility made with the most advanced

techniques. The originality of their methods was striking, and before the later use of overelaborate techniques, their methods were full of a vigor that gave their arts and crafts vitality. Or perhaps the beauty was due to their cultural refinement and well-bred elegance, made possible by much leisure.

Even though most commoners continued to live in a wretched state, the articles necessary for their daily use gradually increased in number. Although only a few of these articles are extant, we can see picture scrolls in which there are assorted objects, such as ironware, tongs (possibly of metal, used for hot charcoal), and long hooks to use over open fires or for hanging flower arrangements, dyed articles, baskets, and bentwood products, which ushered in a new era. Although not yet mature, the objects had an unyielding quality and a feeling of strength and austerity. There is a special quality of beauty found in the articles of the middle ages that was also

136. Andon: *stand lantern. Paper on iron frame; height, 60.5 cm. Eighteenth century. Kyoto. Collection of Kanjiro Kawai, Kyoto.*

characteristic of the applied-art objects of the nobility during the ancient period. The establishment of a system of guilds called *za* not only affected the applied arts of the people but also gave strength and order to the lower classes that were employed as artisans.

Although they were probably well made, the applied-art objects of the upper classes were too artificially elaborate and dehumanized. The division between the fine arts and the applied arts that had started at the end of the ancient period became greater during the middle ages, and by the Edo period (1603–1868) there was a decided separation. Artistic applied-art objects appeared in which a new consciousness of self was expressed. The com-

petition resulting from the independent expression of self-consciousness led the applied arts of the nobility in directions that had no point of reconciliation, and their general decline was one of the characteristics of the Edo period.

Based upon the primitive arts and crafts, there was a blossoming of the common people's applied arts during the Edo period. The orderly and systematic beauty characteristic of the ancient period and the middle ages changed into a beauty redolent of the earth and of sweat. Single-article production ended and many articles were mass produced. All articles used daily by the masses had been called folk utensils, yet these included crudely made articles to which the term should not have

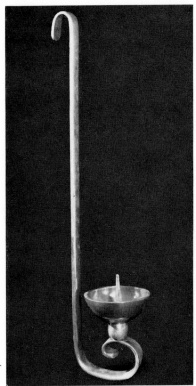

137. Rosoku-tate: *candleholder. Brass; height, 46.5 cm. Nineteenth century. Kyoto. Collection of Kanjiro Kawai, Kyoto.*

been applied. Only those objects that can be treated as applied-art objects can rightly be called folk-art objects.

The most rapid development of folk crafts occurred from the middle of the Edo period onward, and after a period of maturity during the *bakumatsu* era (the end of the Edo period, mid-nineteenth century), it passed its peak of development and followed a downward trend. Various kinds of folk crafts flourished during the Edo period, reflecting the great number of occupations existing among the common people. Beginning with the ancient period and down through the middle ages and the Edo period, folk-craft objects came to display greater gentleness and mellowness, and the forbidding and severe qualities found in objects of the middle ages gradually disappeared. After passing their peak, not surprisingly a facile quality appeared in the folk crafts, though they still retained some of their former features. In the Edo period, glazed pottery, decorated porcelain, lacquerware, and dyed goods became popular, and among woven goods, the making of cloth from *asa* was followed by the weaving of cotton cloth, and even silk was available to a degree. With new techniques of dyeing, stripes could be made, and *kasuri* (woven material with splash patterns) was also used by the common people. There was also the development of furniture decorated with ironwork, especially various kinds of *tansu* (chests).

CHAPTER SEVEN

Influences on the Development of Folk Crafts

PREHISTORIC HANDICRAFTS originated when people made things for their own use, in an age when the head of a family had to build his own house, acquire implements, secure food, and provide homegrown materials for weaving and basket-making, as well as perform other duties. In Africa there are places where men do the weaving, but in Japan women assumed the duty of supplying the clothing while the men made wooden articles, straw raincapes, baskets, and farm implements. The desire to make things for himself is one of man's basic instincts. Even today, almost all the older people of farming and mountain villages in Japan are able to plait baskets or raincapes, because at one time everyone made such things for themselves. This situation is a vestige of the time when the applied arts came into being. People all have different physiques and different movement habits. A specialist craftsman, of course, can make his own tools so as to suit his particular needs. But even a fishing enthusiast living in a city can choose and adapt his angling gear to suit his own needs. In earlier days, this kind of situation was general in most fields of human activity. Before the introduction of money, anyone who could not make something, with the exception of members of the ruling class, could not make a living.

Because hand-made objects were not separated from daily life when they were made in the home,

and as support from family members was the first kind of mutual assistance, the village blacksmith's son wielding a hammer and the daughter-in-law and granddaughter helping with the weaving were common sights. Techniques for making hand-made objects were developed within the family and passed down from generation to generation. Members had to participate in family activities, and children were brought up in an atmosphere where helping at an early age naturally made work a part of their lives. Such was the strict discipline behind handwork, and these were the conditions under which handicrafts developed.

People have never been equal in abilities—there are the healthy and the sick, the physically strong and the weak. And there are differences in intelligence, and differences between people who are skillful with their hands and those who are clumsy. Soon the skillful were making things for the less skillful. Even if an artisan was not able to make something well at first, his craftsmanship improved with experience, and by learning which materials were easy to use and which shapes were strong, the artisan gradually made better, more usable objects. When work proceeded in an orderly fashion, the need for a helper arose because one person could not do all of the work. Although the artisans could learn from practical experience, formal train-

138. Kogatana: *hunting knives. Wood, iron, deer horn, and bone. Length: (above) 24 cm.; (below) 30 cm. Nineteenth century. Japan Folk Crafts Museum, Tokyo.*

ing became necessary, since technology requires specialists with knowledge of various techniques. Thus the conditions necessary for a work system developed. During times when people were laboriously making articles for their own use, they were satisfied if an article fulfilled an immediate need in some fashion. But when work came to be done in systematic ways, the work processes began to gain their own momentum and proceed more efficiently. With the avoidance of wastefulness and the establishment of set procedures, the making of durable, easy-to-use, beautiful objects became possible, and the definition of work, formerly meaning the performance of tasks in the home, was extended. There was a consolidation of techniques, and an element of artistry came to be involved. Cultural customs and manners were reflected in the resulting products, and regional characteristics became manif-

est. These articles, originally folk utensils, came to possess the important element of beauty, and, fulfilling the needs of many people, they became absolutely necessary to community life both regionally and nationally.

The above process explains the birth of the folk crafts and the materialization of folk-craft techniques. Woven materials are especially representative of these beginnings, as woven *asa* and cotton materials were used principally for work clothes. Typical examples include the quilted materials that developed in northern Japan, especially in the Shonai area (in Akita and Yamagata prefectures), the Tsugaru area (in Aomori Prefecture), and the Nambu area (in Iwate Prefecture). Among wooden products, bentwood articles and carved articles for use in the kitchen also developed from such beginnings.

139. O-bachi: *large bowl. Porcelain; 47.5 cm. Seventeenth century. Imari, Saga Prefecture. Japan Folk Crafts Museum, Tokyo.*

THE INFLUENCE OF THE NOBILITY

The common people did not have lives of leisure and affluence. On the contrary, their lot was one of poverty. The kinds of objects used by the ruling class, made with sophisticated techniques from rare materials brought from distant places, were not to be had by ordinary people, however much they might want them. However, once they had attained a little economic stability, it was only natural for them to want to improve the quality of their lives. Not having much creative ability, they could not be expected to start making for themselves objects they had never seen or even heard of until then. They substituted materials that they could easily obtain in large quantities for the precious, rare materials used in making articles for the upper classes, and they simplified the precision techniques of the craftsmen employed by the upper classes. At the same time, they also began to make improvements in the wares they had already been making and using. Since the common people did not have a plethora of master craftsmen capable of executing sophisticated techniques, they could only produce objects that could be made with relatively simple techniques, and since the articles had to be produced in large numbers, not much time could be spent on them. This meant that appreciation by connoisseurs could not be one of the craftsmen's aims. Thus the creation of artifacts that were strong, wore well, and were easy to use—with simplified shapes and decorations—was the special right of

140. Mizu-game: *water-storage crock. Unglazed earthenware; height, 42 cm. Nineteenth century. Oda, Fukui Prefecture. Toyama City Folk Crafts Museum, Toyama Prefecture.*

the common people. The accumulated experience of the demands of their daily lives gave birth to ingenuity and practical wisdom.

Here we see both the cradle of folk crafts and their proper province. They may be lacking in creative ability, they may be imitations of the upper classes—but they are fundamentally different from mere copying. The adaptation of materials and techniques, and the change from the ornamental articles of the nobility to the functional ones of the people, are related to creativity. We may call this change the evolution of nonessential artifacts into essential ones. Or we may say that the condensing and rationalizing functions of technique provide a means whereby a state of free development can be achieved without the loss of unself-consciousness.

In more specific terms, there is a changeover from inhibited, stunting work to a world of spacious freedom. In the case of articles made for the nobility, there was a distance between producer and consumer that disappeared in the popular applied arts. The popular craftsman, having to produce in such quantities that self-consciousness would have made work impossible, was liberated from self-consciousness.

The work of such a craftsman, who was himself one of the people and knew their needs from experience, was merely an extension of the situation where every family manufactured its own necessities. The resulting artifacts, although modeled on aristocratic applied arts, are completely different from these. They are endowed with the strength

141. Mizu-game: *water-storage crock. Earthenware; height, 55 cm. Eighteenth century. Oda, Fukui Prefecture. Toyama City Folk Crafts Museum, Toyama Prefecture.*

142 (*opposite page, left*). Hana-ike: *flower* ▷ *vase. Earthenware; height, 26 cm. Eighteenth century. Naeshirogawa, Kagoshima Prefecture. Kumamoto International Folk Crafts Museum, Kumamoto Prefecture.*

143 (*opposite page, right*). Hana-ike: *flower* ▷ *vase. Unglazed earthenware; height, 31.7 cm. Eighteenth century. Yokino, Kagoshima Prefecture. Kumamoto International Folk Crafts Museum, Kumamoto Prefecture.*

characteristic of folk crafts and of the common people themselves.

Folk-craft objects tended to imitate the upper-class forms and structures of the previous generation. Examples of this include the change from embroidered to stencil-dyed kimonos, the simplification of patterns in *inaka yuzen* (a gaily patterned, painted silk material), and the modification of *maki-e* (lacquerware in which lacquer, mixed with colored powder, silver, gold, and tin, is used to paint the design) into *e-urushi* (a strong black lacquerware decorated with red and gold flecks). The artisans, instead of making handcarved decorations that required much time and special techniques, adopted stencils. They no longer drew detailed designs but made simple patterns, and they also used *imban*, woodblocks, for printing designs. Since the common people employed the same techniques for weaving silk material that they used in weaving flax and cotton material, the silk that they made can be classified as a folk product. One reason for the development of the applied arts of the common people was that some kilns in the daimyos' fiefs were no longer under the patronage of the fiefs after the beginning of the Meiji era, and came to be operated by the common people.

IMPORTED CULTURE Every culture is influenced by cultural exchanges and importations. Just as ripples move outward when a stone is thrown into a pond, any given cultural trait is certain to spread. Buddhism

began in India and went to Japan via China and Korea. When it came into direct contact with the peoples of these countries its nature changed. Due to recent technological advances the spread of a cultural trait is no longer determined by the time factor. Now it is possible to come into immediate contact with other cultures, whereas in the past it took so long for cultural exchanges that an element arrived not in its original state but in a changed form.

Culture from abroad was transmitted and spread either by the upper classes or by the lower classes. Buddhism is a good example of a cultural element that originated in the upper classes and took many years to penetrate the thinking of the common people. Another example is *kasuri,* which came to the Ryukyu Islands from the south during the Edo period. *Kasuri,* its use limited through clothing regulations and by the tax system, was made into material only for the kings and nobles. It had no bearing on the lives of the common people, who comprised seventy percent of the whole population, until after the Meiji era. Clothing regulations were then abolished, enabling the common people of Okinawa to use *kasuri* freely. During the middle of the Edo period (ca. 1730) *kasuri* entered Kyushu via Satsuma (an earlier name for Kagoshima Prefecture), and from the start it was a popularly used material for the clothing of the common people.

Kin karakawa, embossed leather goods decorated with gold, were made in Himeji (a city in Hyogo Prefecture). The techniques for making *kin karakawa*

144. Kago: *basket. Bamboo and hemp-palm rope; height, 41 cm. Twentieth century. Amami Oshima Island, Kagoshima Prefecture. Kurashiki Folk Crafts Museum, Okayama Prefecture.*

were imported from western Europe from the end of the Muromachi period through the Momoyama period (1568–1603). Because leather was related to fighting equipment, *kin karakawa* were used to decorate objects that symbolized the samurai. A decrease in the demand for personal effects and military wear by the upper-class samurai made more of these objects available to the common people. Other influences from abroad included Western-style painting, using perspective and shading, which influenced the *doro-e* paintings (Figs. 93, 94, 132). Woven material called *tozan* (a cotton material with striped patterns, first imported from Holland) was used by the samurai when it first reached Japan, later by Kabuki actors, and finally by the common people. It spread throughout the land, stimulating home-weaving as it did so. Various techniques were spread throughout the country

during the Edo period by pilgrims traveling to the Ise Shrine (in Mie Prefecture), the so-called Eighty-eight Temples of Shikoku, and the Kotohira Shrine (Kagawa Prefecture, Shikoku), dedicated to the deity Kompira. The dissemination of *kasuri* and striped patterns certainly proceeded along these routes.

ECONOMIC FACTORS Applied arts, of whatever type, necessarily have an economic aspect. Even at the stage where every family manufactured its own necessities, when there was a little time to spare, extra articles would be produced, and these could then be used for bartering. Once social institutions such as the Muromachi-period guilds, or *za*, were established, craftsmen began to work within these economic organizations.

145. Ramma: *transom. Wood and bamboo; 40.6 × 132 cm. Eighteenth century. Takayama, Gifu Prefecture. Kusakabe Folk Crafts Museum, Gifu Prefecture.*

146. Ki-zara: *wooden dish. Length, 27.6 cm. Nineteenth century. Hokkaido. Collection of Keisuke Serisawa, Tokyo.*

The Edo period was the golden age of folk crafts, with all kinds of wares produced throughout the country. Each fief of the feudal system then in force was a self-sustaining economic unit. At the same time, free trade was gradually increasing, and goods had begun to circulate through the land. There were, thus, two different economic systems existing side by side. Soon the economic spheres of small regions were penetrated by merchandise produced on a large scale. Unable to keep up with the competition, many industries received special protection, since the necessities of life had to be furnished from within each area. The people within an area were hired to do the work, but often when the need arose, artisans were also hired from other areas. When a daimyo was transferred from one fief to another, the craftsmen working in an occupation receiving special protection always accompanied him to the new fief. Artisans were encouraged to make improvements in their various crafts, and those who did so were exempted from taxes and from forced labor. Some were given allowances and residences. The merchants of the areas where special industries were located had the right to publicize their wares by making presents to the shogunate and to daimyos, and in addition they had direct privileges in connection with passage through border checking posts and restrictions on the movements of artisans. A few of the many products having commercial value that developed under such conditions were the paper stencils of Shiroko, Mie Prefecture, the tie-dyed cloth (Fig. 36) of Narumi, Aichi Prefecture, and the leather goods of Kofu, Yamanashi Prefecture.

Before the Edo period there were occasionally persons of high rank who were defeated in battle

147. Hoso-obi: *sections of narrow undersashes. Cotton. Nineteenth century. Okinawa Prefecture. Japan Folk Crafts Museum, Tokyo.*

and went to remote areas to live. Although when these people had been in the capital they had never done any manual work, in such reduced circumstances they had to do something in order to stay alive. Some of these people started making the artifacts they had enjoyed using when they were prosperous. There are many instances of such work becoming hereditary in a family and eventually receiving protection as a rare craft. Barkwork (Figs. 77, 78) and hand-made paper are representative examples, and there are similar instances in the fields of ceramics and lacquerware. It was only natural that the merchants, as middlemen who promoted the growth of demand, should begin to wield great power. Apart from articles like tools, which were an extension of the daily necessities manufactured by a family for its own use, trade in applied-art objects came under the economic control of the merchants. On the one hand this meant a stable livelihood for the artisans. On the other hand, with the development of mechanized industry mass-producing cheap goods,

craftsmen were forced to lower their standards. They were eventually forsaken by the merchants, and their crafts started down the road to extinction.

GEOGRAPHIC FACTORS   At present there are many synthetic materials, and efficient transportation systems allow delivery of these materials from their place of manufacture to any area. Production is carried out in areas with favorable working conditions, good power sources, and a large supply of labor. But when the applied arts first developed, there were no synthetic materials, and because the natural resources close at hand had to be depended on, early articles reflected the characteristics of those regions in which they were made.

Through their varied climates and natural features, geographical environments foster different ways of life, so that no two areas are exactly the same. The vegetation found in the northern hemisphere is different from that found in the southern hemisphere, and the vegetation of the

148. Futamono: *covered bowl. Earthenware; height, 19 cm. Twentieth century. Shinano, Aichi Prefecture. Collection of Shoji Hamada, Tochigi Prefecture.*

dry and wet areas of the temperate zones are also different. There are many differences between the environments found on continents and on islands, on plains and in mountain areas. There are also very clear differences between the kinds of life that exist in oceans and in rivers, or on land and in oceans and lakes. Geologically, too, there are differences. For instance, there are no iron-ore deposits in the Tokyo area, but there are in the Tohoku area of northern Japan. It is because of such geographical differences that the applied arts of various districts did not develop along the same lines. In areas without iron ore and sufficient fuel resources, metallurgy is impossible, and whereas bamboo wares were plentiful in Kyushu and Shikoku to the south, bamboo crafts did not develop in the Tohoku area in the north. Again, since cotton cultivation is not feasible in northern or mountain districts, cotton textiles did not show much progress there.

Let us take ceramics as another example. In Seto (near the present Nagoya), pottery and porcelain have been produced in large quantities since the Heian period (794–1185), mainly because of the great quantities of high-quality clay that can be found there, and because the nearby mountains contain ample supplies of iron oxides. Moreover, there are also deposits of an ore called *yama-gosu,* which contains natural cobalt, and this is one reason why the first decorated porcelain in Japan was made in Seto. In a location like Seto, therefore, this work naturally flourishes, and this means that many people gather to participate in the work. Division of labor takes place—clay digging, firewood chopping, throwing pots on the wheel, decorating, kiln packing, stoking, transport. Thus specialists are born, techniques are refined, the artisans become organized, and wages and prices are stabilized. With the passage of time a tradition evolves. More high-quality, reasonably priced goods can be produced than in other locations. These are the kinds of multiple conditions that enabled Seto wares to spread throughout the eastern part of Japan. In the Kanto district the word *seto-*

149. Dobin: *teapot. Earthenware; height, 12 cm. Eighteenth century. Kuromuta, Saga Prefecture. Collection of Shoji Hamada, Tochigi Prefecture.*

mono (Seto wares) came to mean "ceramics." In the Kansai district (the Kyoto-Osaka area), the word *karatsu-mono* (Karatsu wares; named after Karatsu City in Saga Prefecture, Kyushu, which was the distribution center for these ceramics) was similarly used to mean "ceramics." Similarly, the porcelain ware produced in northern Kyushu is called Imari. This type of porcelain is fired in the many kilns centering on Arita City, and the name is taken from the port of Imari, from which this porcelain was first shipped. Both Arita and Imari are located in Saga Prefecture.

In the field of the applied arts, it is customary to refer to articles by the names of the places in which they are produced. There is *kihachijo,* woven on Hachijo-jima, an island lying to the south of Tokyo. *Yuki* is a kind of *tsumugi,* or silk homespun, distributed from Yuki in Ibaragi Prefecture. The same is true of *hakata* (silk material made in the city of Hakata in Fukuoka Prefecture,

Kyushu), *kokura* (cotton material made in Kokura, Fukuoka Prefecture), *oshima* (*tsumugi* made on O-shima Island, Kagoshima Prefecture), *ojiya* (crepe from Ojiya, Niigata Prefecture), and *kurume* (*kasuri* from Kurume, Fukuoka Prefecture, Kyushu).

In the case of folk crafts, it is no exaggeration to say that the quality of the materials used determines the quality of the finished product. The good quality of Ojiya *chijimi* (Fig. 46) is due to the high-grade ramie grown in the Aizu region of northern Japan. Because this area lies in the greatest snow belt in Japan, it is possible to bleach the material by putting it out in the snow during the humid winter. Differences in the quality of the silk, wool, cotton, and *asa* fibers show up clearly in the finished products, and the same holds true for the materials used in making metal, glass, and wooden goods. The key to the development of many applied-art objects can be found in the geographical conditions of the region.

CHAPTER EIGHT

Recent Changes in Folk Crafts

FOLK ARTIFACTS are embodiments of the life styles of the common people. Thus an understanding of the kind of life the people of a particular region lived can be gained by examining the folk articles of that district. From tableware we can learn about eating habits, and clothes reflect the climate and also the working environment. Because local differences in customs become firmly rooted through time and because of differing geographical conditions, each region has special characteristics. Folk artifacts reflect these differences and the characteristics of the regions in which they are made. The common people required durable goods, and this requirement brought about a simplification and condensation of techniques.

In folk artifacts we can see a simple beauty unlike the beauty of articles made for the nobility. The artisans who made the folk articles had no self-consciousness. They had a sense of discipline, a sincere feeling of humanity, and a sense of community that enabled them to protect their traditions. Lack of self-consciousness did not mean that the artisans lacked awareness of their feelings, thoughts and impressions, but it meant that an artisan spirit with an emphasis upon absolute sincerity was fostered. Obstinacy was also there, but this was essential for the preservation of traditions, for the evaluation of the finished products, and to prevent disorganization. Moreover, in handwork, the feelings of the artisan unconsciously affected his work and the artisan in turn was also affected by the artifacts that he was creating.

Today, economic pressures tend to break down this spirit of the artisans. Folk artifacts prior to the industrial revolution were reasonably priced handmade objects. Making things by hand was the only method of production, and the objects were never of poor quality. In folk crafts, although simplification and development of techniques seem at first glance to be self-contradictory, they are actually in accordance because human beings, though full of contradictions, attempt to achieve integration. Basically different techniques are used in making folk articles, as opposed to those used for machine-made objects. Machines set up restrictions preventing any deviation from set plans, so that the resulting sense of beauty of its products is quite different from that of folk articles.

THE NEW FOLK CRAFTS   Articles for the new times began to be made around 1926 in the Shimogamo area of Kyoto, and later in Tottori and Shimane prefectures. In Shimogamo the movement was centered on a group of artists; in Tottori a number of people who advised the craftsmen were the moving force. In Shimane, however, it was the craftsmen themselves who grouped together. Thus the three groups were rather different in character, but one point all three had in common was the fact that they kept in close touch with and constantly received advice from Soetsu Yanagi, the prime mover in the folk-

art movement, and the artist-potters Kanjiro Kawai and Shoji Hamada. From the outset, the new folk crafts not only adapted to the changing times but were innovative, too.

The movement spread to the pottery town of Mashiko in Tochigi Prefecture, Toyama Prefecture on the Japan Sea, Matsumoto in Nagano Prefecture, Hirosaki in Aomori Prefecture, Kurashiki in Okayama Prefecture, Okinawa, and Iwate Prefecture. Different specialties arose: ceramics, weaving, dyeing, wooden artifacts, lacquerware, metalwork, paper products, etc.; and the artists, artisans, and advisers kept in contact with one another, so that these specialties developed as one chain of activities. The new folk crafts, modeled on earlier folk traditions, and receiving support from people with deep knowledge and technical competence, made rapid progress. From the start there was a conscious, intellectual element involved, and the work lacked the unself-consciousness of the traditional folk crafts. The craftsmen were eager to understand and preserve the spirit of the old folk crafts and had the ability to eliminate their shortcomings. But their strengths were at the same time weaknesses, for the craftsmen were inevitably governed by the patterns they had followed in the past, and the new age called for folk wares designed to meet the requirements of new life styles.

Kanjiro Kawai and Shoji Hamada, who together with Soetsu Yanagi were the leading spirits of the new folk-craft movement, were pure artists rather than craftsmen, and we do not need to consider their work here. Other artist-participants in the movement include Keisuke Serisawa, Kichinosuke Tonomura, Yoshitaka Yanagi, Michitada Funaki, Kenkichi Tomimoto, the English potter Bernard Leach, and Tatsuaki Kuroda. These are all individual artists and their works, of course, are not folk crafts. They are the products of their individual wills and capacities. In the sense that they adopted the good points of traditional folk crafts, they may be said to be in the same position as craftsmen of the new folk crafts, but in fact their position was that of leaders and advisers. The products of the new folk crafts were directly influenced by these artists. Old folk crafts (including still surviving

◁ *150 (opposite page, left).* Bon: *tray. Lacquer over wood; diameter, 27.3 cm. Nineteenth century. Yoshino, Ishikawa Prefecture. Collection of Kichiemon Okamura, Tokyo.*

◁ *151 (opposite page, right).* Haze-tsubo: *pot for catching goby fish. Unglazed earthenware; height, 21.7 cm. Nineteenth century. Okayama Prefecture. Kurashiki Folk Crafts Museum, Okayama Prefecture.*

152. Tsubo: *crock. Earthenware, height, 20.3 cm. Seventeenth century, Seto, Aichi Prefecture. Collection of Shoji Hamada, Tochigi Prefecture.*

traditions), new folk crafts, and the work of artist-craftsmen, are generally confused, but their beginnings and the attitudes of these people toward their work are all different. Naturally enough, their creations also display these differences. The three are closely related, and superficially it seems to be possible to treat them as one, but in fact there are clear differences.

THE ERA OF HANDWORK

All people and all events are influenced by the changing times. There are peaceful eras and dark, sad eras. The desires and the will of the individual usually are of no avail. No matter how a person may long for peace, as an individual he is helpless to change the conditions of the age, and no one can ignore the circumstances in which he lives. The applied arts, too, have been influenced by the changing times.

As mentioned earlier, folk artifacts are products made by hand before the influence of mechanization became too great. Just when an interest in folk art was developing during the Taisho (1912–26)

and the early part of the Showa (1926–present) eras, great changes began taking place that would influence the materials, techniques, shapes, colors, marketing, prices, and basic feelings of both the artisans and consumers.

Although machine-made products became popular, about half of the goods sold in stores at this time were still handicrafts. Thus there was no particular need to use the word "hand-made." With just a little care and effort, it was possible to indulge tastes that would be extravagant by today's standards. There were plenty of craftsmen with a mastery of the traditional techniques who would willingly undertake work and carry it out faithfully, just as the old craftsmen had done. They did not begrudge time or trouble, but on the contrary were grateful for the chance to do the work they were accustomed to, and to make a satisfactory job of it. The artisan's conscience—the dread of a shoddy job—was still strong. Business dealings were carried on in good faith, and prices were incredibly low. Indeed, hand-made products were usually cheaper than machine-made ones. Today, such a situation

153. Zushi: *miniature shrine. Unglazed earthenware; height, 24.5 cm. Twentieth century. Kuwayama, Kagawa Prefecture. Kumamoto International Folk Crafts Museum, Kumamoto Prefecture.*

seems too good to be true, but we must remember that these were the last stages in the decline of the handicraft tradition. There were fewer machine-made goods on the market than hand-made ones, and people somehow thought that machine products were better. In fact people had a tendency to look down on the hand-made objects they were accustomed to. This is yet another example of a phenomenon common to all mankind—the eternal hankering for new things.

Expressions like "it looks as if it's been made by machine" were used to describe a neat, accurate finish and were intended as praise, even in an age when machine-made things were no longer so rare. The artisans fought against being displaced by machines by making their wares to the best of their abilities and selling them at low prices.

FOLK CRAFTS AND WAR During the Taisho and early Showa eras, folk wares were still being used by older people, who were accustomed to these utensils and because there was still a definite demand for objects with regional characteristics. Also, the artisans who engaged in making these folk articles, unable to adapt themselves to the new life styles, continued to make things just as they had always done. If they had been clever they would have broken away from the outdated craft traditions even earlier. The beauty of the surviving traditional folk crafts, however, does not lie in cleverness. It is a beauty sustained by the sincerity of tradition. But the young people had no interest in making things just as they had been made in the past. The artisans who did persist with this work gradually grew old

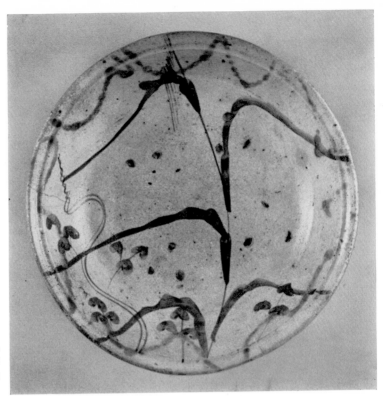

154. Sara: plate. Earthenware; diameter, 31 cm. Seventeenth century. Kasahara, Gifu Prefecture. Japan Folk Crafts Museum, Tokyo.

and died, and the number of products steadily diminished. From about 1939, then, these folk artifacts suddenly lost their vitality, and following the Pacific War their numbers continued to decrease.

In times of war, all the scientific and technological resources of a country are mobilized for the development and manufacture of equipment and supplies needed for the war. War brings about advances in science, but it also ravages a country's resources. And the same thing happens to man's spirit. It is no exaggeration to say that World War II dealt a fatal blow to handicrafts.

Many people lost virtually everything during the war, and for a time immediately after the war families were doing handwork to produce clothes and utensils for their own use, since neither the depart-

ment stores nor local shops had any merchandise worthy of the name, and anything that was made for sale sold out immediately. Handwork, already fatally wounded by the war, was finished off by the vacuum of the immediate postwar period. Those folk crafts that were survivals of the traditional crafts suffered the greatest damage, for the modes of life on which these crafts depended were changed completely by the war.

FOLK CRAFTS ESTRANGED FROM DAILY LIFE

As time passes new generations arise. Some people wanted to revive such tradition folk crafts as were still surviving, some just wanted to get on the bandwagon. Some business-minded people and young people made "tradition" and "regional color" their

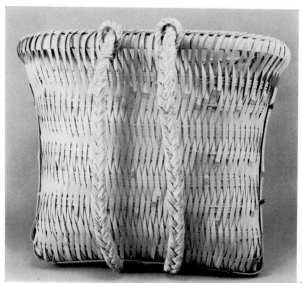

155. Shoi-kago: *basket carried on the back. Bamboo and straw; height, 34.5 cm. Twentieth century. Takachiho, Miyazaki Prefecture. Kurashiki Folk Crafts Museum, Okayama Prefecture.*

slogans. Old craftsmen who had almost resigned themselves to their fate were at a loss to understand why people were fussing over them again, and remained half-sceptical. Some may have been happy at the arrival of this "folk-craft boom," but the firm foundations that had been buttressed by the old style of life were no longer there. Unfortunately, too, the pleasure of handwork and fame were very often in conflict.

Early in the Showa era, some people found it necessary to talk about the value of folk crafts because they felt they had a duty to make this buried treasure public. The situation after the war, however, was quite different. There was an illusion that anything made by hand was to be respected. Today, more than twenty-five years after the war, there is no longer anyone who tries to oppose machine production with handwork. Machine production and handwork have come to have distinctly separate roles. Handwork has long lost the popular quality of folk craft, and its products are gradually becoming the possessions of a privileged class, similar to the applied arts of the nobility of earlier

times. People who make straw raincoats and hats go out into the fields wearing machine-made raincoats, and they cover their heads with sheets of plastic. The old ways of life that were common when the word *mingei* (folk crafts) first came into use no longer exist. Nowadays, objects that can be properly called folk-craft products are to be found only in out-of-the-way places. Folk crafts have become merchandise sold as local souvenirs, estranged from people's daily lives. In fact, when people in country towns talk about "making *mingei*," they actually mean making souvenirs for tourists.

Some handwork developed in other directions. When craftsmen started to aim at "appreciation" by connoisseurs, their work turned into what might be called "elegant wares," which people delusively thought were of a higher class than souvenirs. In the Meiji era, when the prefectures were established in place of the old feudal system, some of the former fief pottery kilns fell into private hands and started producing wares for the tea ceremony and flower arrangement. Many of the items we see labeled as folk-art products are in fact "elegant wares." The so-called folk artifacts that are used as tableware and souvenirs at restaurants are sometimes criticized for their self-conscious pseudo-simplicity, and there is a tendency to extend this criticism to all folk crafts. But this is not valid, for it is a misapprehension to think that anything made by hand is folk art.

Although the time will come when the meaning of the word *mingei* will be clarified, it does not seem possible while this generally used term continues to take on even more meanings. The age when the meaning of *mingei* was readily understood has passed. We now live in an age where it is difficult to work collectively, since each individual takes responsibility for his own livelihood and works according to this premise. Even though some folk crafts are accorded protection by being designated Intangible Cultural Properties, the more conscientiously an artisan does his work the harder his lot is. Such difficulties can only be overcome by the individual's willpower and abilities. When we consider that the best work today is being done by artists rather than craftsmen, we can see how difficult a true craftsman's work is.

We can probably find some fine folk crafts still surviving if we look around for them. But they are probably destined to fade away soon, or to undergo radical changes.

I would like to say a word here about the term *mingei-sakka* ("folk-artist"). "Folk craft" and "artist" are not really compatible terms. In fact, inasmuch as folk crafts arose in answer to the needs of society as a whole, and the artist is motivated by a desire to express his individual will and ability to create, the two are diametrically opposed. Even if folk artifacts and the works of an individual artist show similarities of dimension, color, and design, it would be a mistake to regard them as the same. To make a compound noun out of these two incompatible words is completely meaningless.

The indiscriminate use of the word *mingei* in all kinds of unsuitable combinations is perhaps another sign of the times, and shows up the facileness of most people's thinking about folk crafts.

CHAPTER NINE

The Folk Crafts Today

SCIENCE AND MAN   We are living in the twentieth century. With the development of air travel, the globe seems to be shrinking day by day, and the sense of distance has become almost nonexistent because of the diffusion of radio and television. This is the age of science. Particularly since the end of World War II, science has made tremendous progress and our lives owe a great deal to it. In fact it is impossible to conceive of life without it.

The war stimulated the development of science, and though civilian needs were met only after satisfying those of the military, convenient consumer goods were produced by applying methods originally developed for military purposes. And after people began to use these articles there was less demand for the products of the surviving folk crafts, which were more suited to the traditional modes of life of former periods. After the war, synthetic fibers greatly influenced the field of textiles, polyethylene bags replaced tubs, barrels, jars, and the like as containers for foods, and the spread of simple running-water installations made water-storage jars unnecessary. Science is breaking down the differences between city and country life.

Science made possible the development of machines for mass production, and the standardization of materials and manufacturing processes brought about vast quantities of standardized products. Workers do not handle the products directly, the only requirement being that a close watch be kept over meters and gauges. Machines operate according to set plans and produce the same article over and over again. Being based on knowledge shared by the whole world, machine-made articles show a uniform monotony on an international scale. It is not only distance that is done away with by science. Differences in kind also disappear.

Although machine-made products are the result of the application of mankind's knowledge and unsparing efforts, in terms of beauty, unfortunately, they fall far short of man's requirements. Although the knowledge used has been gathered by warm-blooded human beings, the results are cold and insipid. The development of science has undeniably brought great blessings to the human race, but at the same time it mercilessly eliminates human qualities. The emotional element that people never cease to seek is missing. This is why there is so much controversy about "human beings versus science." Take, for example, ferro-concrete apartments, representative of modern architecture. Although they are earthquake-proof, fireproof, designed to save space, and conveniently equipped with heating and air-conditioning systems, there is something about them that fails to appeal to the human heart. On the contrary, these apartments, planned for comfortable living, have an alienating effect. Even the potted plants lined up along the verandas look sad. There are also the synthetic materials that are moth-proof, lighter than wool, soft to the touch but stronger than steel. There is the "no-iron"

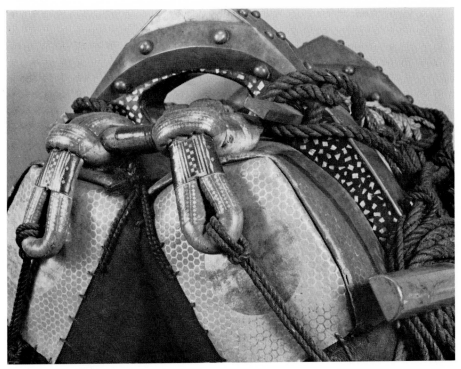

156. Ni-gura: packsaddle. *Height, 51.5 cm. Twentieth century. Tochigi Prefecture. Collection of Kanjiro Kawai, Kyoto.*

apparel that can be washed in the evening and is ready for wear the next morning. Less than a generation ago, synthetic fabrics like these were inconceivable. Moreover, the synthetics can be made to resemble wool or silk. Yet, if we read between the lines of all the publicity about the "scientific" advantages of synthetic fibers, we find that they have lost their nature as fibers. If synthetic fibers are ten times finer, more durable, more uniform, and stronger, why is there still a demand for natural silk? We can only say that it is because synthetic fibers are dead.

MACHINE PRODUCTION Chemistry is representative of a world without sentiment; its strength lies in standardization and uniformity. But nature and people are neither standardized nor uniform. That is why silk, *asa,* and cotton fabrics, each with differing characteristics, came to be made and used. It is undeniable that these natural fibers have both merits and weaknesses, but their merits are numerous enough to make up for their weaknesses. In fact, by trying to eliminate the weak points one inevitably sacrifices the very qualities that are their essence. A rational, efficient plan for eliminating all that is unnecessary restricts the human heart. There are times when the useless is not wasteful, when it is necessary and serves a purpose.

The low prices characteristic of machine-produced goods are achieved through mass production and the use of huge quantities of raw materials. Even if the raw materials are synthesized chemically, their constituents have to be taken from

157. Kyosoku: *armrest. Wood; height, 30.6 cm. Nineteenth century. Collection of Kanjiro Kawai, Kyoto.*

nature, and usually from underground resources. There is a limit to the resources that lie buried in the ground, and even if they are used economically, huge amounts are consumed. Once these underground raw materials are used up, they cannot be replaced. Human rationality seen from this viewpoint does not make sense at all. The indiscriminate excavation of underground resources is robbery and plunder, it is the same as resorting to violence; arrogance is probably the best word for this.

It is impossible to ignore developments in science, and, like it or not, our daily lives depend on science. But many question whether science as it is now is a good thing or not, and since scientific advances are made each day, questions concerning what di-

rection it will take are of great importance. Unsound scientific progress that endangers human existence and runs counter to the will of the human race must be rejected. Science has great value and must be respected, and because of its value we must be cautious. The material needs of life are being met, but people feel an emptiness. What does the single flowerpot on the windowsill of an apartment mean? What do the weekend trains filled with young mountain climbers mean? People are seeking the tranquillity of nature to ease the anxiety arising from their dissatisfactions. Seeking repose in nature is related to the longing after one's hometown, because people originally lived in natural surroundings and grew up receiving the benefits of

158. Tsuitate: *single-panel screen. Wood and bamboo; height, 73.5 cm. Nineteenth century.* Collection of Kanjiro Kawai, Kyoto.

nature. Science lacks this hometown-like feeling, and since the impulse to return to nature is a very human desire, rationalization is not always beneficial.

Utensils of various kinds help people to live the kind of life they want, and the use of utensils is man's distinguishing characteristic. Utensils are extensions of the human body, clothes are extensions of the skin, chopsticks are extensions of the fingers. Because man's tools and utensils are extensions of his body, great care went into their making. Man looked to nature for his materials, and made his artifacts with his hands. Although inconvenient for handling hard, heavy, or hot objects, man's hands respond sensitively to his will. Thus hand-made artifacts embody both nature and man's will, for in them natural materials have been shaped by man's needs. The value of tools lies in their capacity to transmit the subtle movements of man's hands and feet. And machines, it is true, represent a further development of tools, but unfortunately they operate outside the sphere of man's will. The autonomy possible with tools disappears. The modern thirst for handwork is simply a manifestation of the desire for this autonomy.

IRREGULARITY Natural materials are not uniform. From bottom to top, front to back, each filament of an *asa* plant differs in hardness and tensile strength. The outer and inner

159. Yu-gama: *pot for heating water. Iron; height, 21 cm. Nineteenth century. Kanaya, Aichi Prefecture. Tottori Folk Crafts Museum, Tottori Prefecture.*

layers of a cocoon are dissimilar. The quality of clay varies according to where it is dug. This means that these materials had different uses inherent in them from the first. Irregularity means adaptability. A lack of homogeneity is valued because irregularity is possible. Nature aims to create diversity, and human beings are unable to do anything about this lack of uniformity—a silk strand is thick in some places and thin in others, and its tensility varies along its length. Despite efforts by human beings to try to make the strand uniform, the natural irregularities remain. Nature does not want to alienate man from itself; it wants to preserve a close relationship.

Man's will has two aspects: systematization and expansion. Removal or systematic ordering of irregularities corresponds to systematization, while making use of irregularities as they are corresponds to the expansion aspect. Plain, unpatterned cloth represents the former, while *kasuri* cloth and *namako* (a blue-green glaze with white spots) wares or accidental firing effects represent the latter, and are examples of irregularity promoting techniques. An extreme emphasis on either orderliness or development is in direct opposition to nature, and because nature is more powerful than human beings beauty results from adjusting to nature.

Human beings require periods of rest from activity, or in other words, they need irregularity. When the hand-operated potter's wheel is turned, it spins rapidly and then slows down. Hand-spun thread is made in segments no longer than an arm's length, and the thread is at rest while the fixed lengths of spun thread are being transferred to

160. Oke: *tub. Wood, bamboo, eggshells, and lacquer; height, 25.5 cm. Nineteenth century. Kyoto Prefecture. Tottori Folk Crafts Museum, Tottori Prefecture.*

reels. Thus, in handwork it is possible for the worker to snatch intervals of rest. There is a lack of systematization, and the work progresses by means of both quick and slow repetitive movements. Human nature avoids restriction, so high value should be attached to this lack of uniformity. It is unwise for the small ego of human beings to reject nature's assistance, since nature offers a lack of uniformity so that human beings may find rest and comfort.

FOLK ARTIFACTS AS DAILY COMPANIONS As mentioned before, the plastic arts began with handwork, stemming from the need for clothing, food, and shelter. The further back one goes in history, the less people interfered with nature, and the beauty of early artifacts, stemming from harmony with nature,

was based on this noninterference. By expressing their egos and thus working independently, the artisans in effect turned against nature. This resulted in a differentiation between beauty and ugliness, and the divergence of the fine arts and the applied arts. Expression of the ego was necessary in the evolution of the human species, and though the fine arts definitely expressed the will of the people, because the fine arts depend on the ego and represent the beauty of the ego, their beauty is of a very individualistic nature. Such beauty has value, but the ego does not represent the human personality in its entirety, and furthermore, the expression of an individualistic style in the applied arts weakens the solace offered by nature. Because handwork requires a cooperative form of living in which harmony is a fundamental characteristic, and because the beauty of the applied arts is a beauty that stems from the tranquillity offered by nature, people must live in mutual cooperation with one another and with nature. It is no wonder that people long for folk artifacts in our present competitive age, when these qualities are in such short supply.

Since utensils are so important for daily life, there is nothing as unfortunate as a lack of serenity or ease. Even if people are not always conscious of the dreariness of their life and of its uniformity, there is a troubling insecurity deep in their hearts. The search for something meaningful manifests itself as a single pot of flowers, or in the act of climbing a mountain, or as the purchase of folk artifacts to be added to one's furniture. The era in which handwork alone fulfilled specific human needs has long since passed, and in all likelihood such a period will never appear again. To completely reverse our machine culture back to handwork not only is im- possible but would be pointless. But handwork should not be thought of as merely something that recalls the past. Hand-made objects reflecting the tranquillity of nature give sustenance to troubled spirits. Despite the pressure of work and daily living, human beings still ardently desire to improve themselves, and to desire hand-made articles is to respect both human beings and nature. I do not mean that all hand-made objects are beautiful, nor do I mean that all folk articles are beautiful nor that folk-craft articles are the only articles that offer comfort. But in order to live fully, people must find spiritual satisfaction. Because many people seek such spiritual comfort in folk articles, which embody this comfort in the most simple, concrete form, I am angry about the poorly made articles that are sometimes called folk articles, and my heart is heavy when I think about the sad realities of human nature, with its reliance on reason and its conviction that science is omnipotent.

TITLES IN THE SERIES

Although the individual books in the series are designed as self-contained units, so that readers may choose subjects according to their personal interests, the series itself constitutes a full survey of Japanese art and will be of increasing reference value as it progresses. The following titles are listed in the same order, roughly chronological, as those of the original Japanese editions. Those marked with an asterisk (*) have already been published or will appear shortly. It is planned to publish the remaining titles at about the rate of eight a year, so that the English-language series will be complete in 1975.

The "weathermark" identifies this book as having been planned, designed, and produced at the Tokyo offices of John Weatherhill, Inc., 7-6-13 Roppongi, Minato-ku, Tokyo 106. Book design and typography by Meredith Weatherby and Ronald V. Bell. Layout of photographs by Sigrid Nikovskis and Ronald V. Bell. Composition by General Printing Co., Yokohama. Color plates engraved and printed by Mitsumura Printing Co., Tokyo. Gravure plates engraved and printed by Inshokan Printing Co., Tokyo. Monochrome letterpress platemaking and printing and text printing by Toyo Printing Co., Tokyo. Bound at the Makoto Binderies, Tokyo. Text is set in 10-pt. Monotype Baskerville with hand-set Optima for display.